NATURE'S ABSTRACT

ADULT COLORING BOOK

KYMIE EDWINS

NATURE'S ABSTRACT: Adult Coloring Book

www.KymieEdwins.com

Book Cover Design by www.coveratelier.com

ISBN-13: 978-1517230791
ISBN-10: 1517230799

WELCOME TO NATURE'S ABSTRACT

This coloring book contains 50 black and white floral and nature abstracts for your coloring pleasure. You may use any coloring materials you wish.

ABOUT THE AUTHOR

Kymie Edwins is a Creative Director based in New York City. Aside from watching Broadway Musicals, she spends her time saving the world one pixel at a time, or at least that's what she thinks.

http://www.KyimeEdwins.com

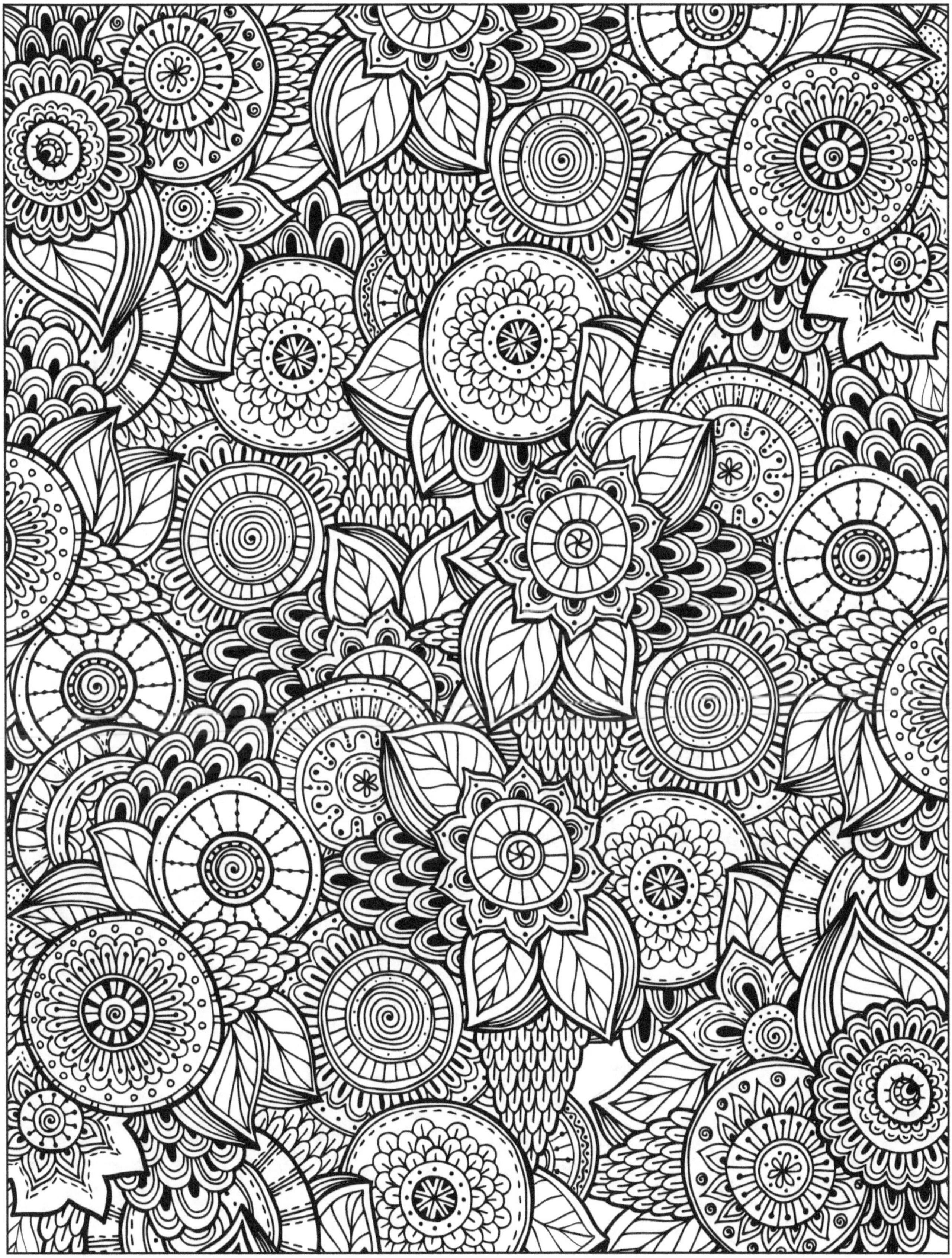

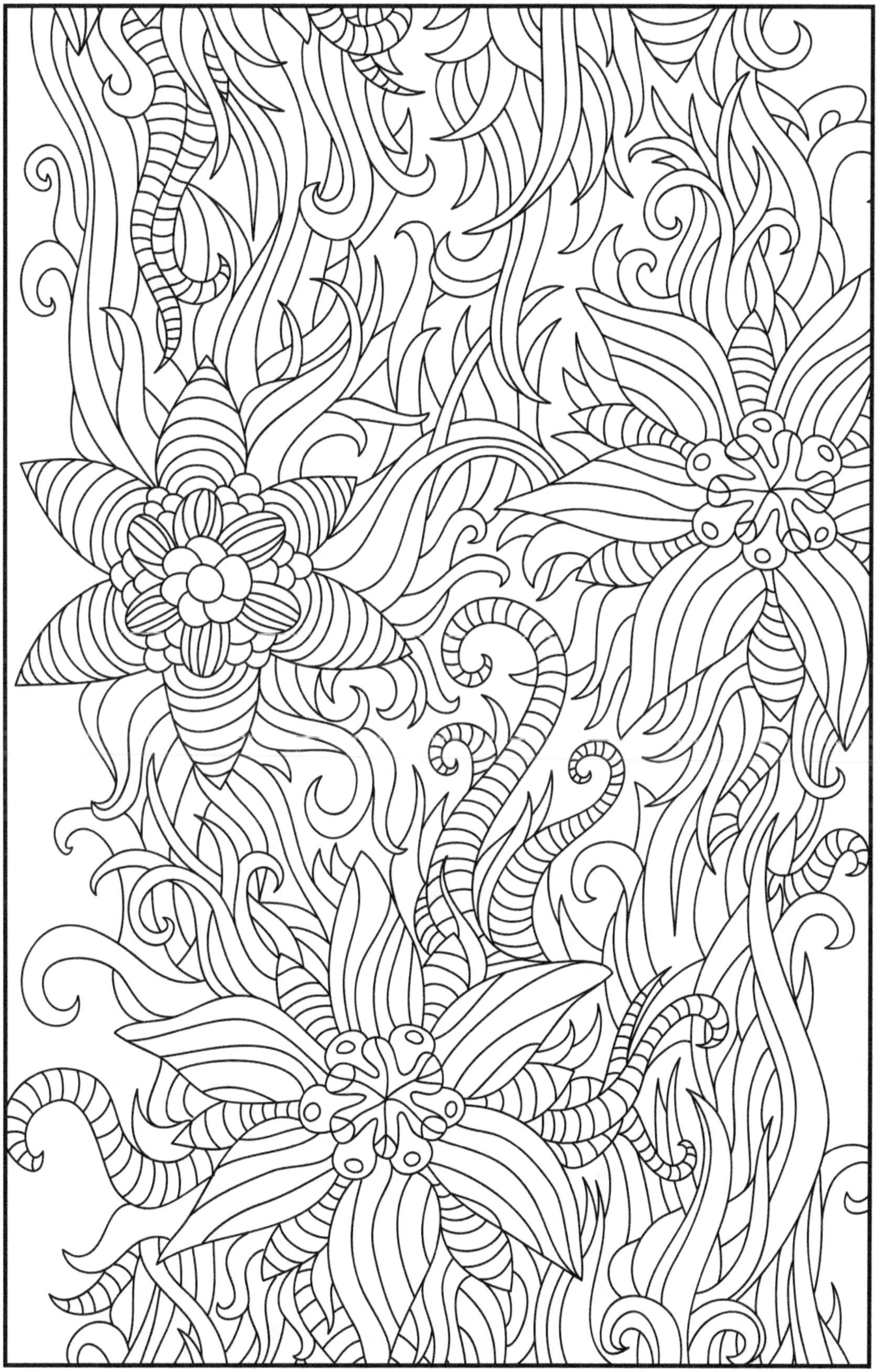

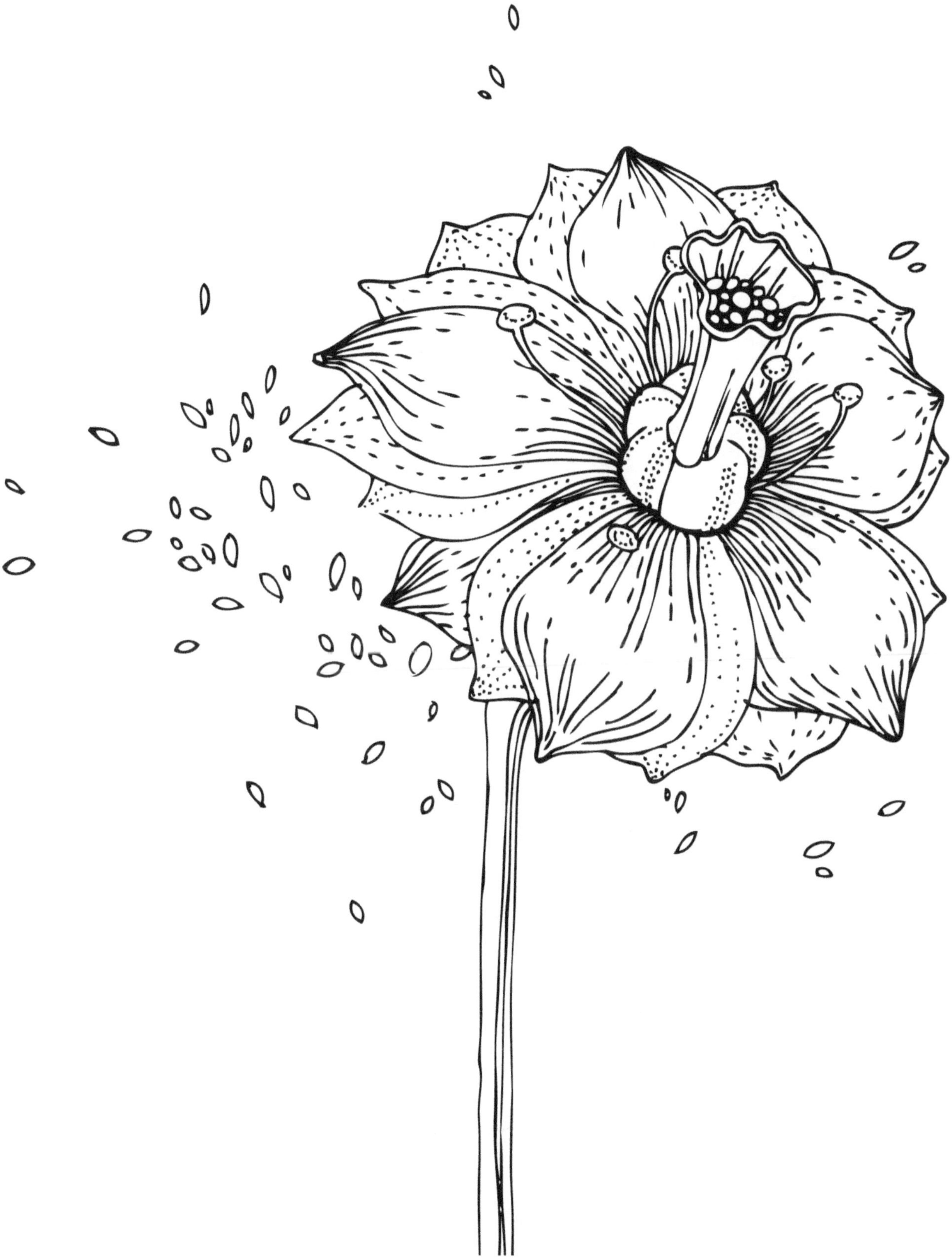

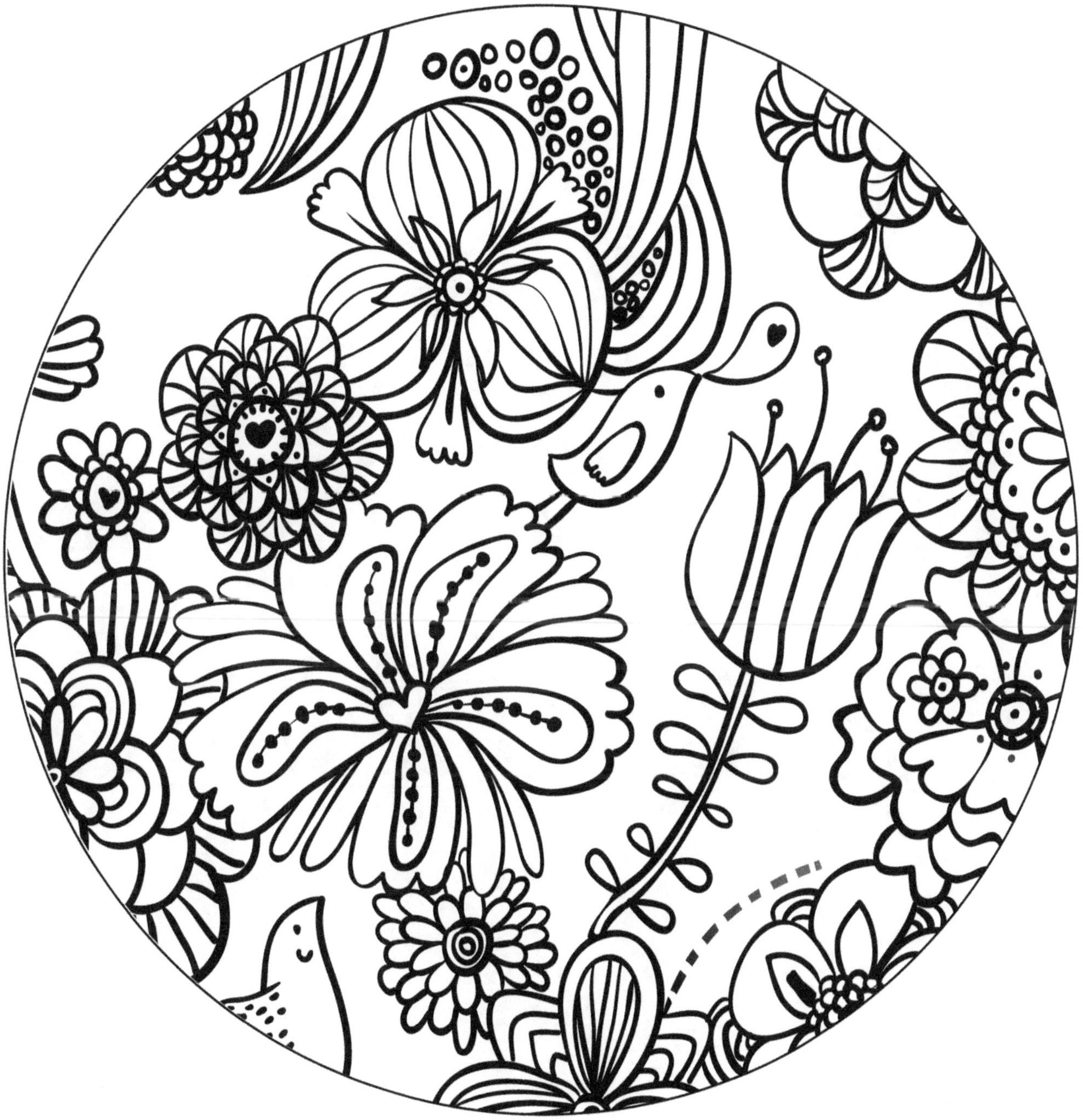

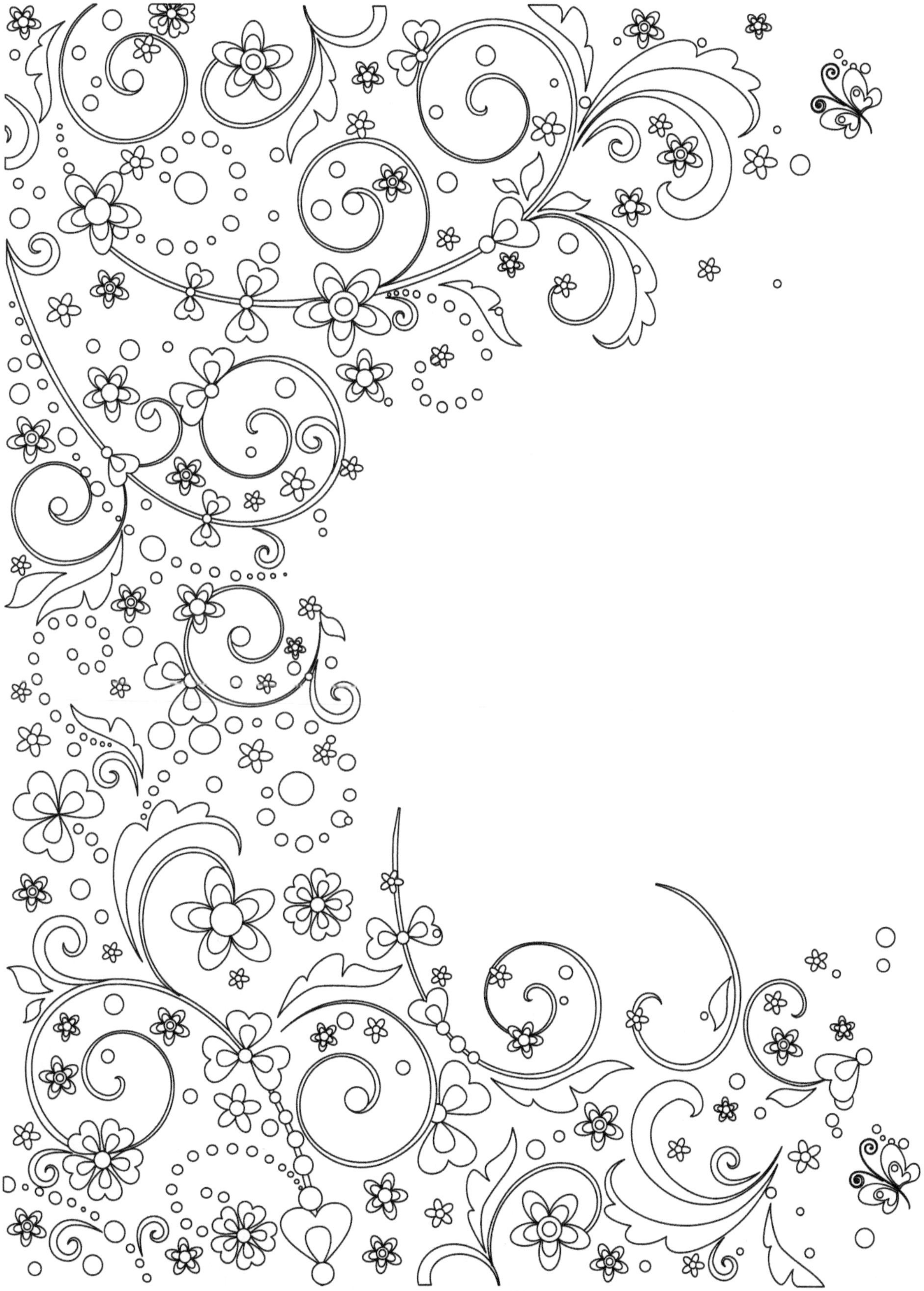

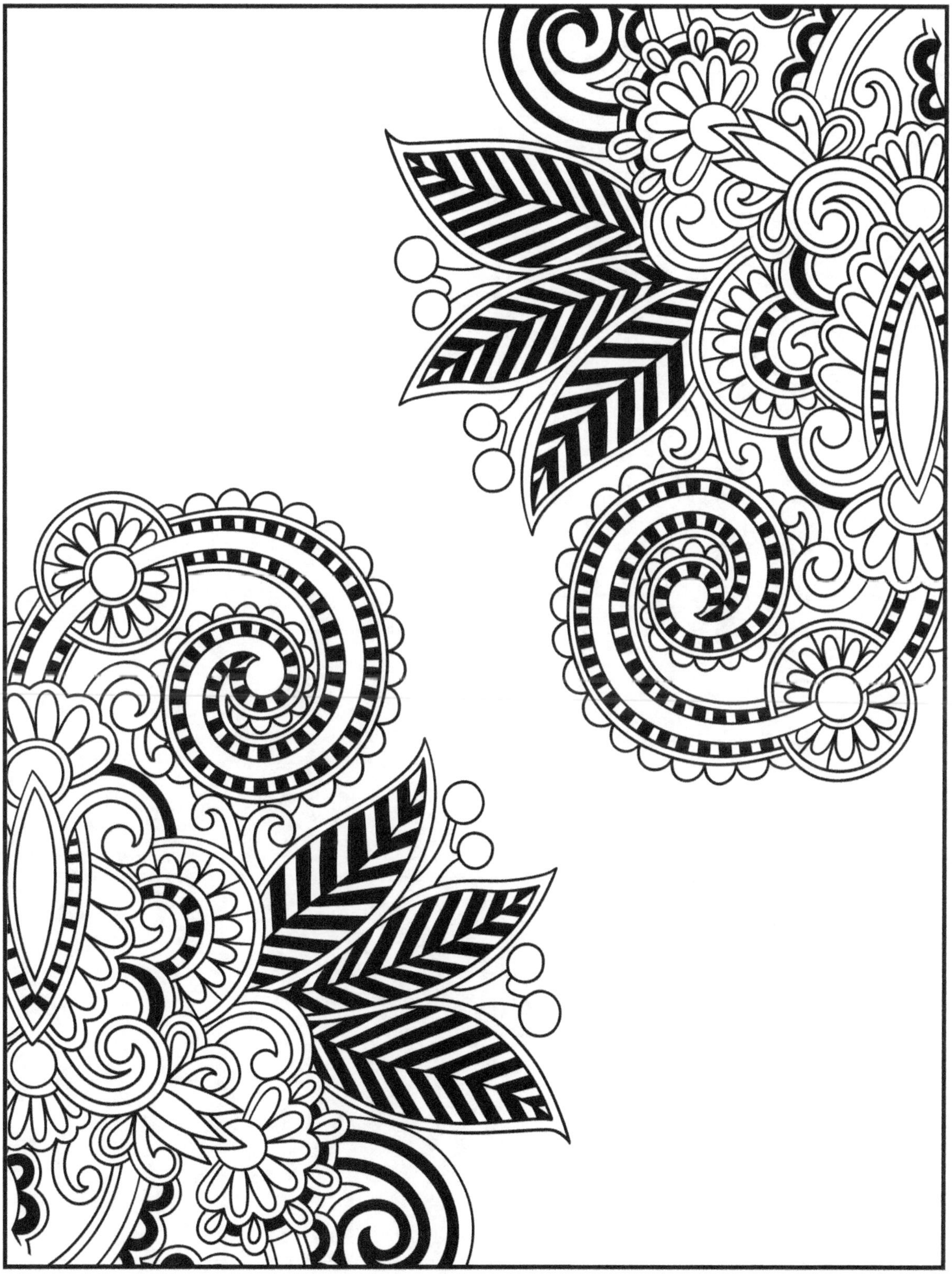

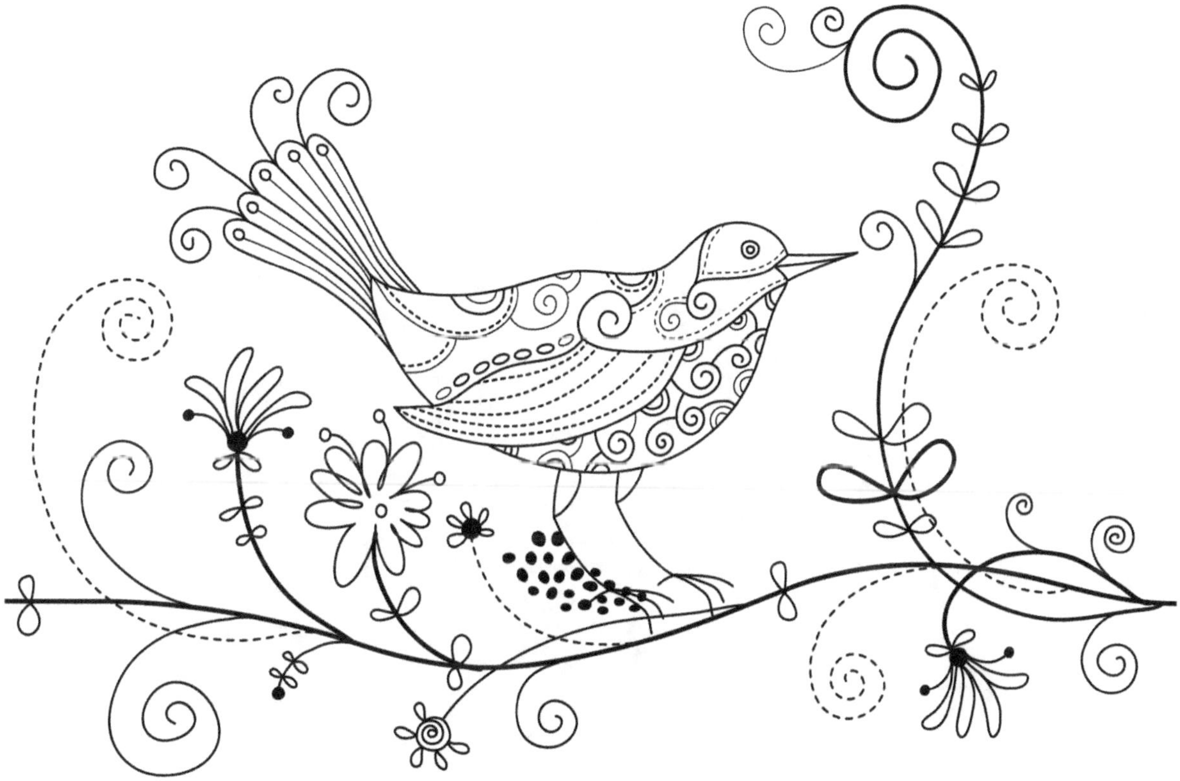

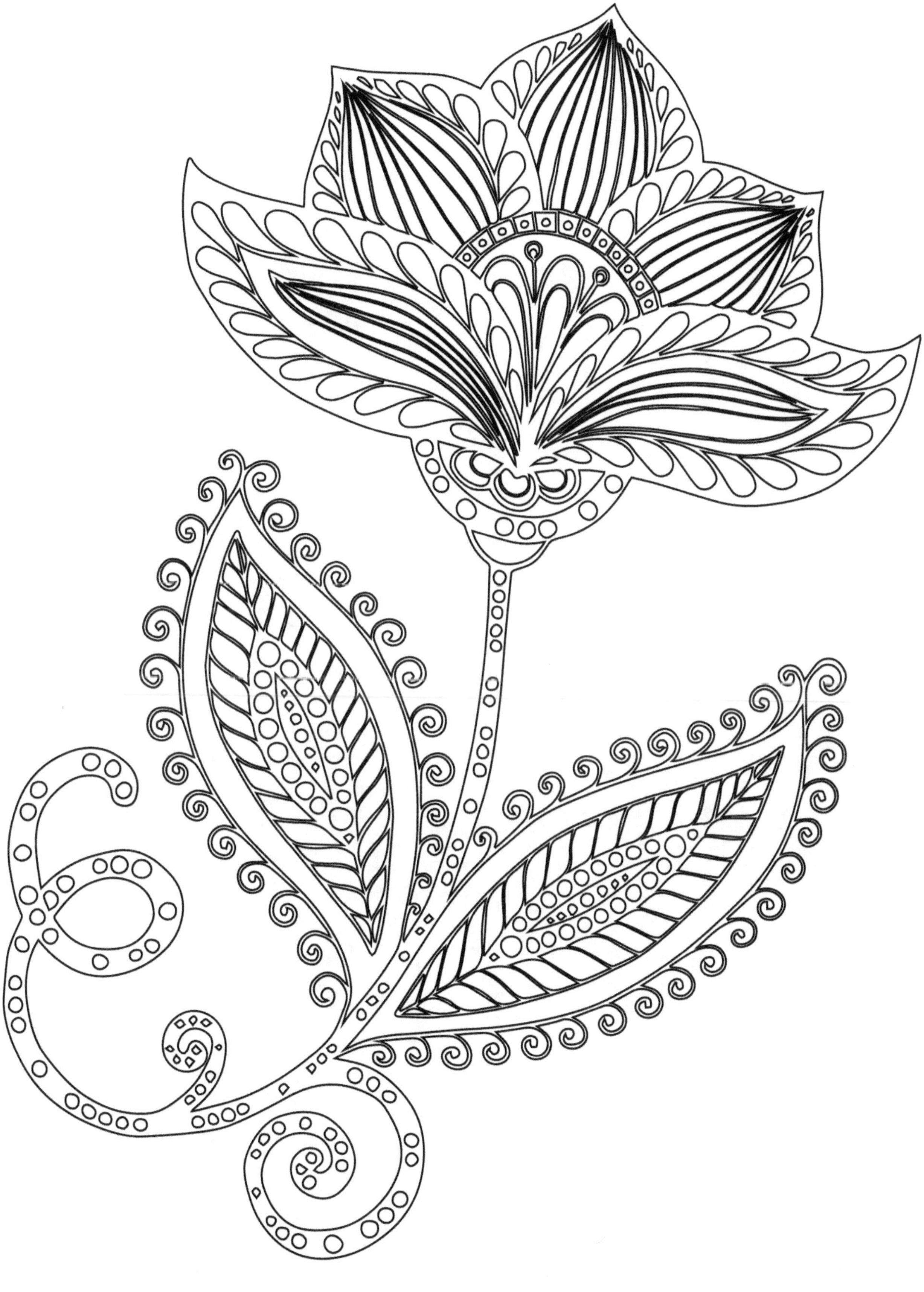

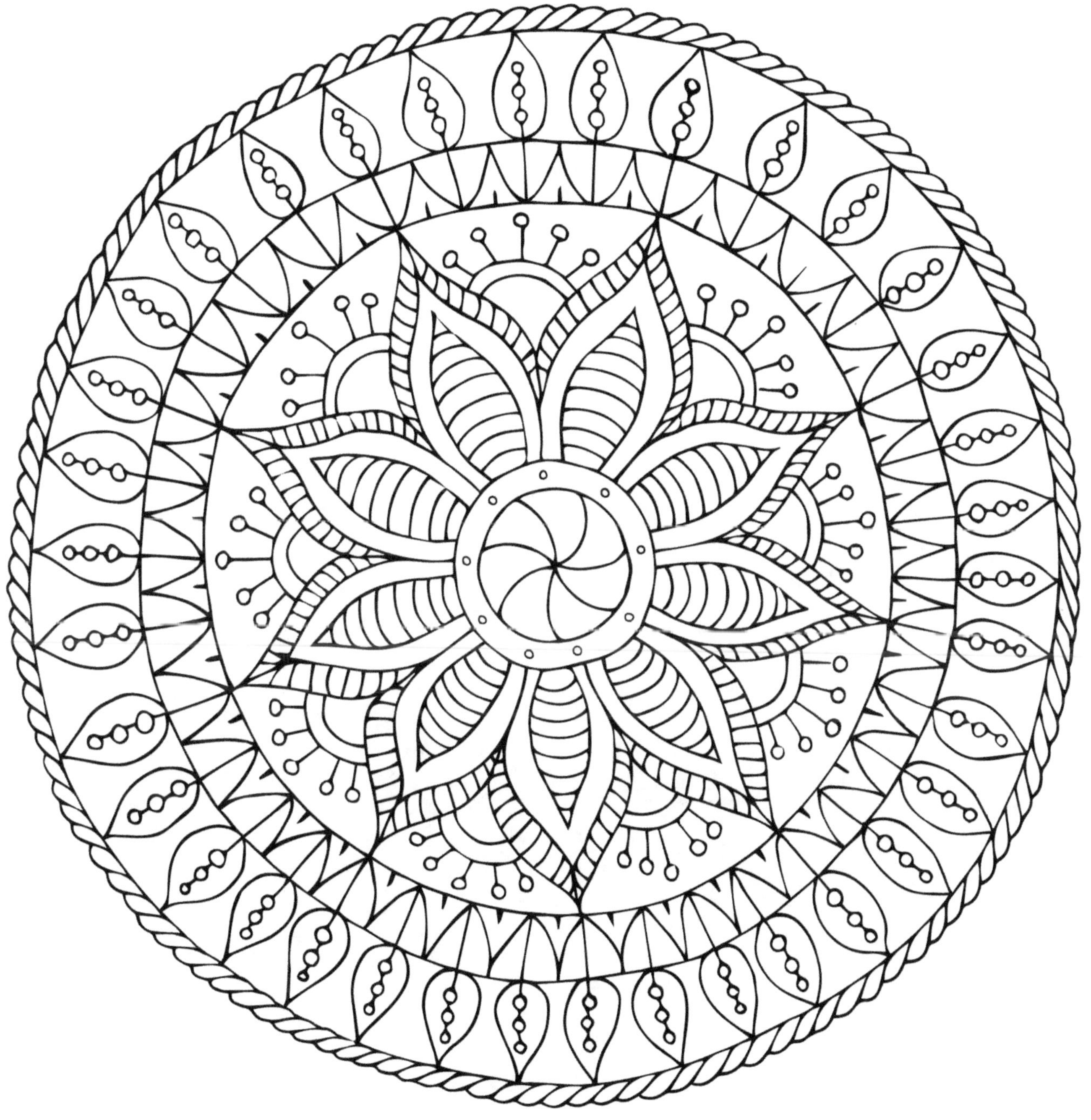

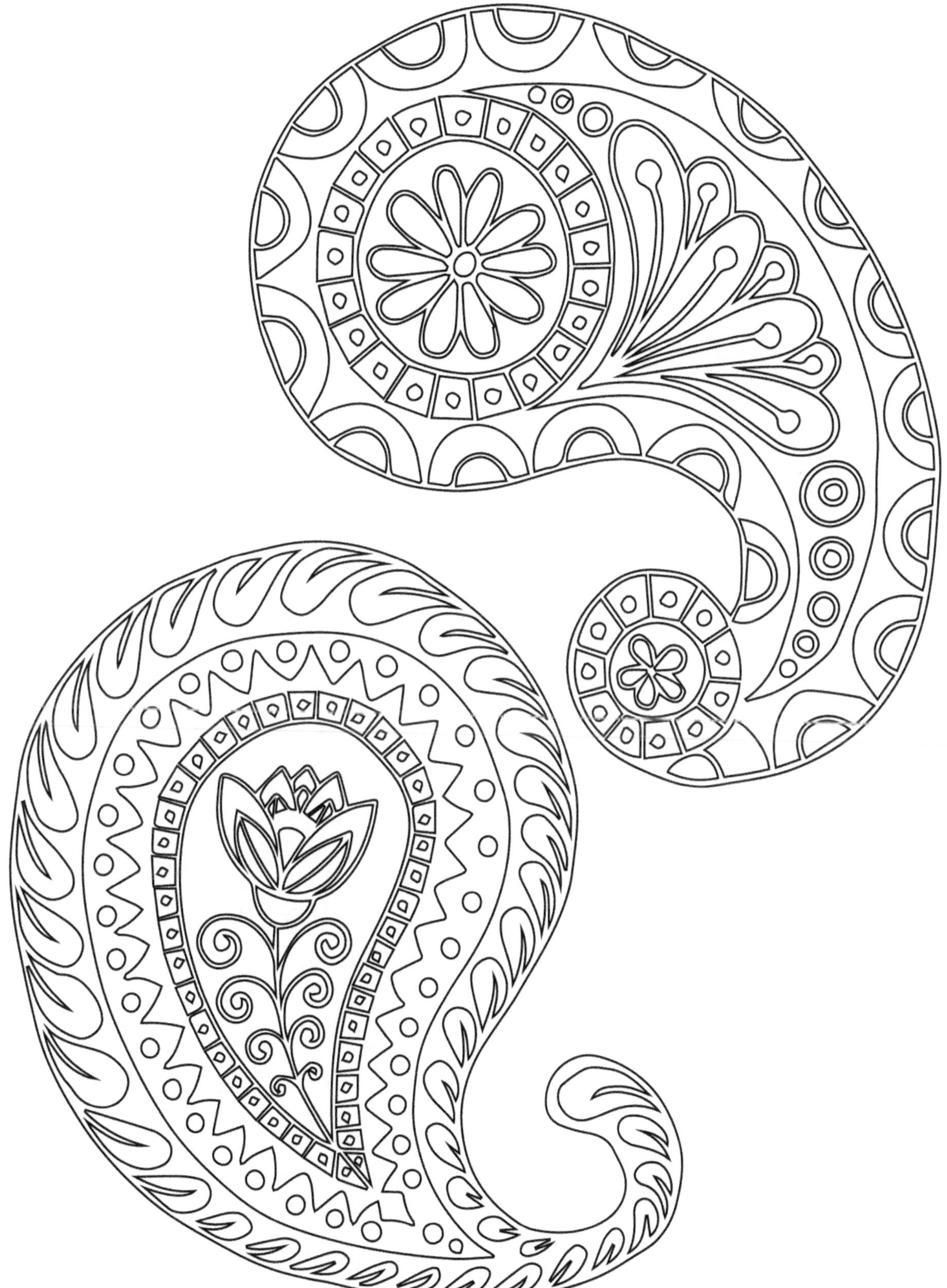

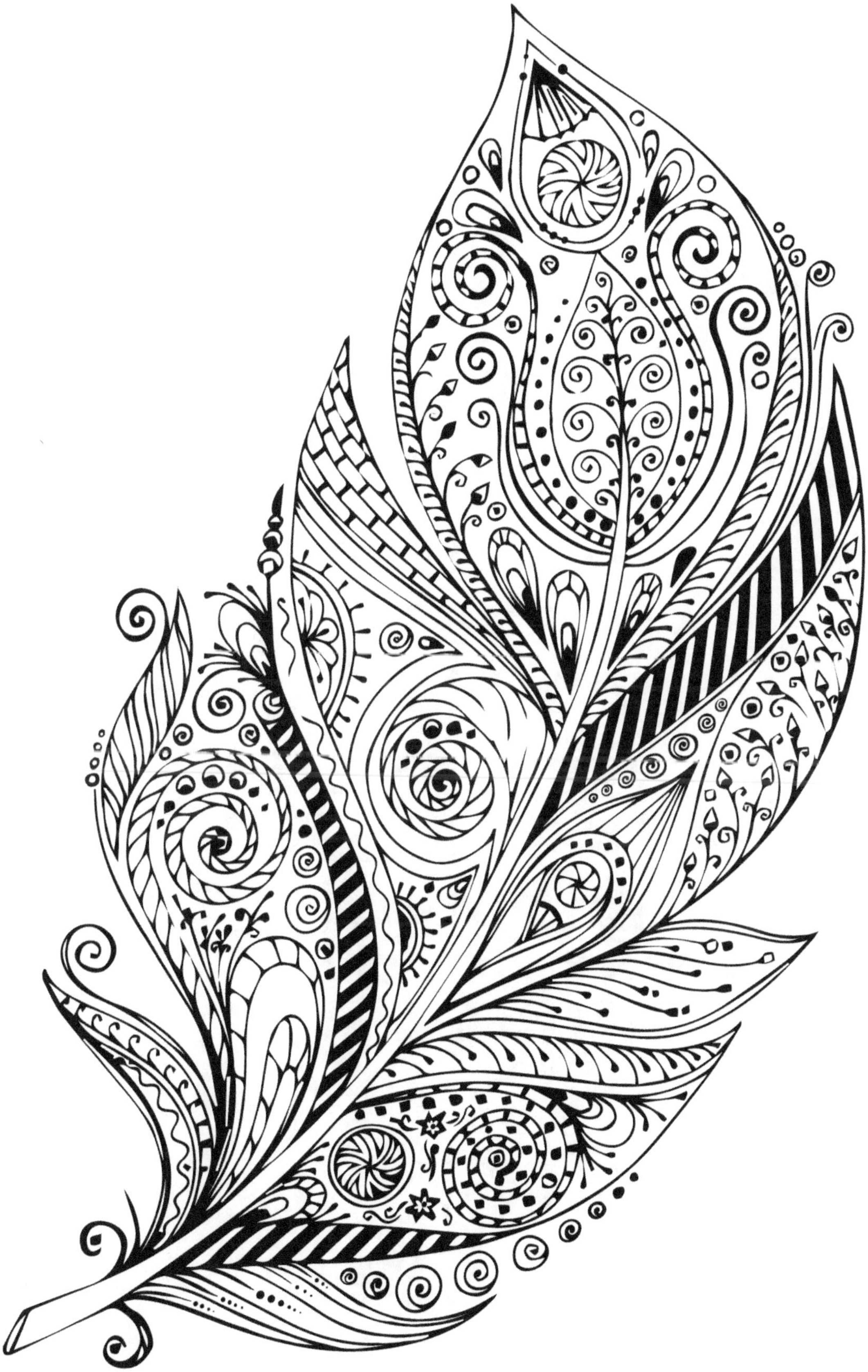

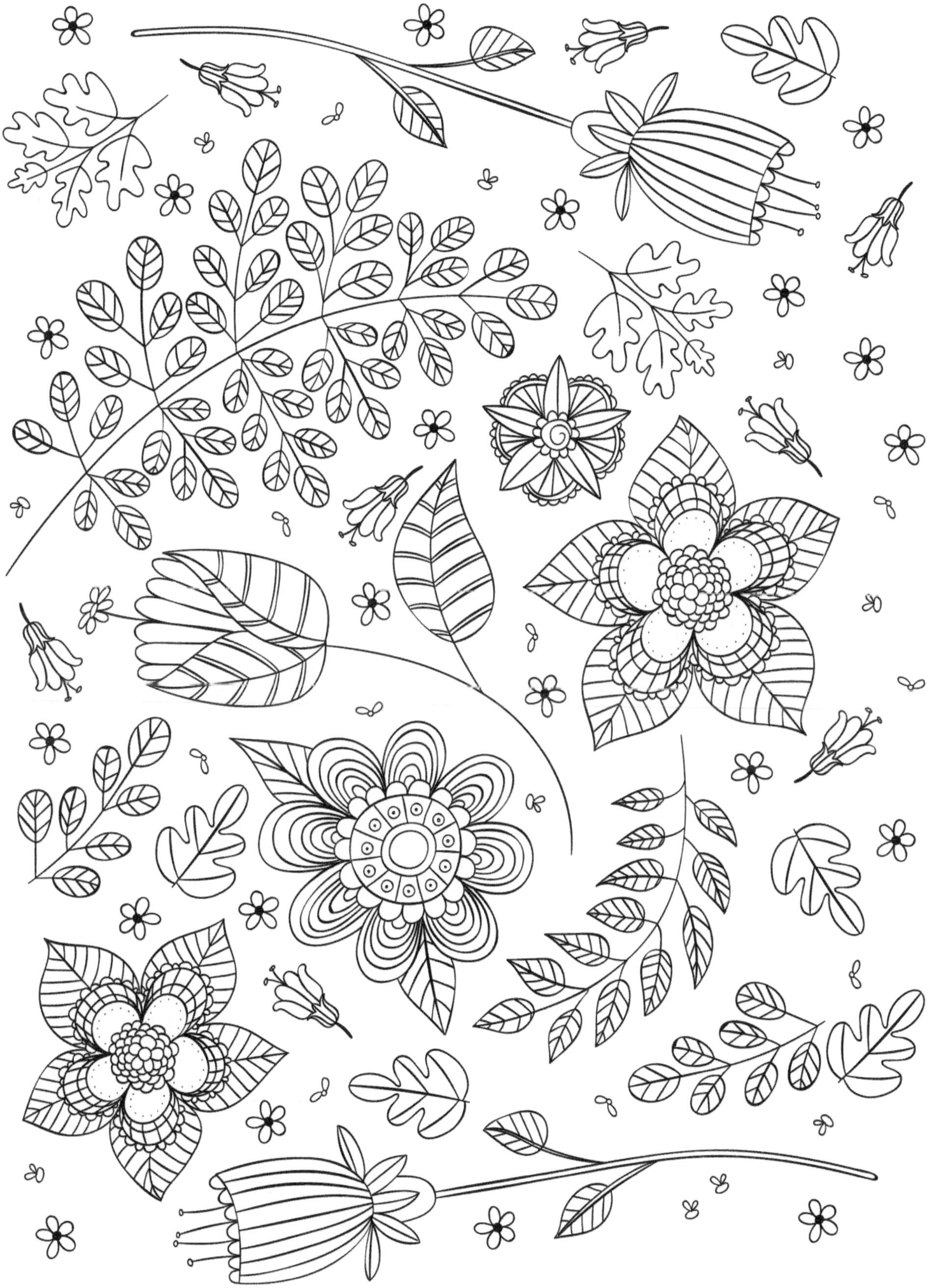

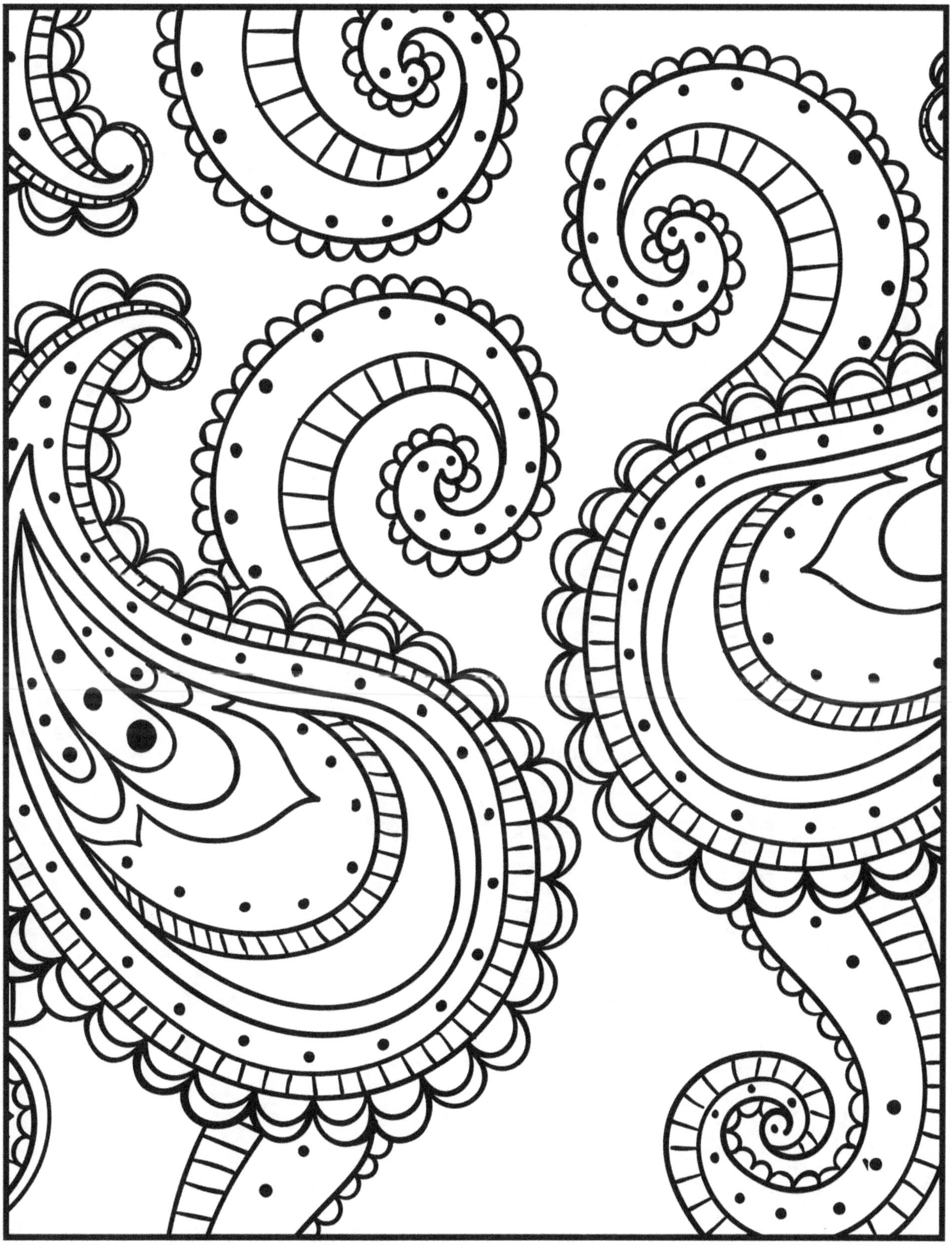

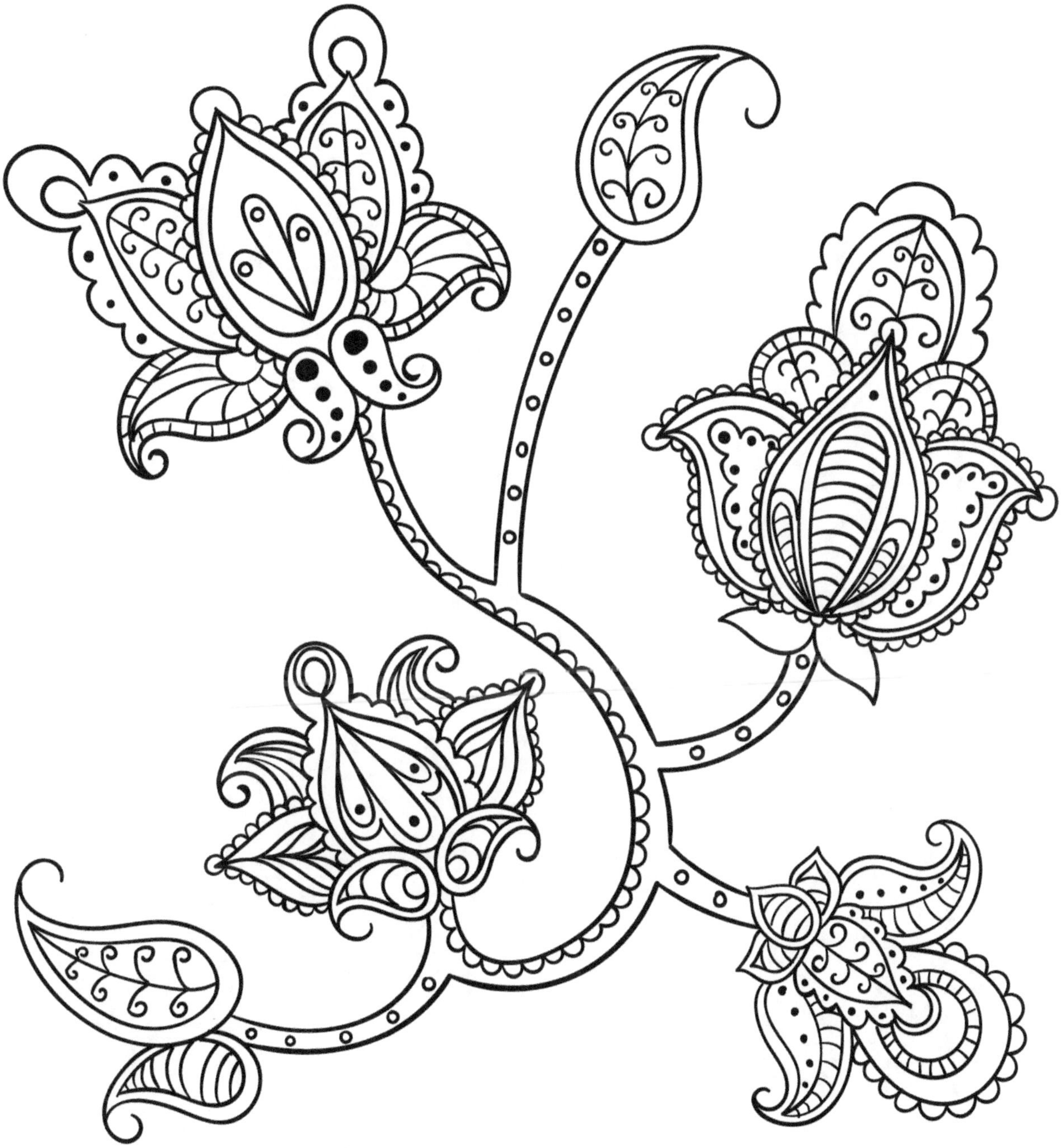

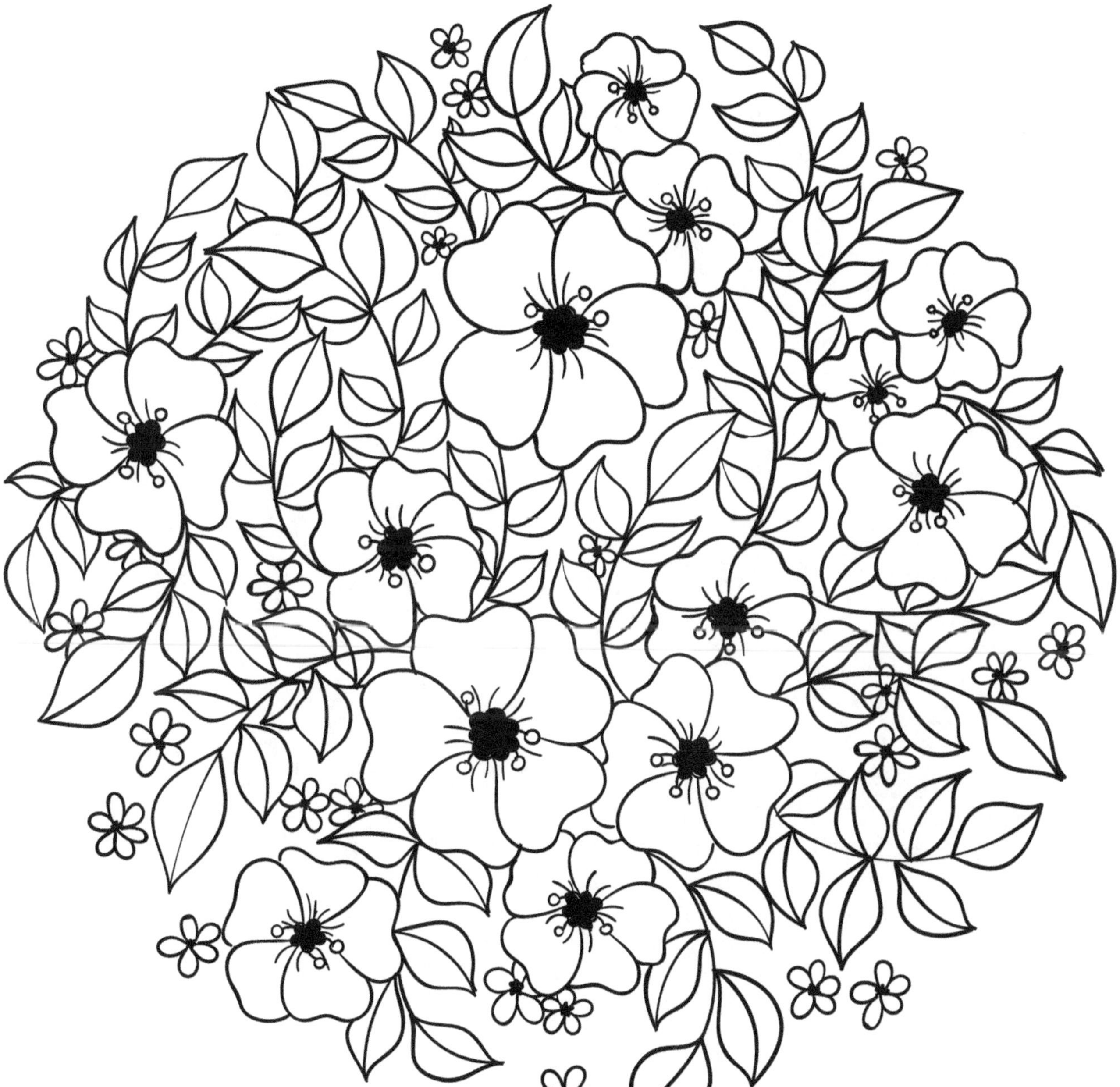

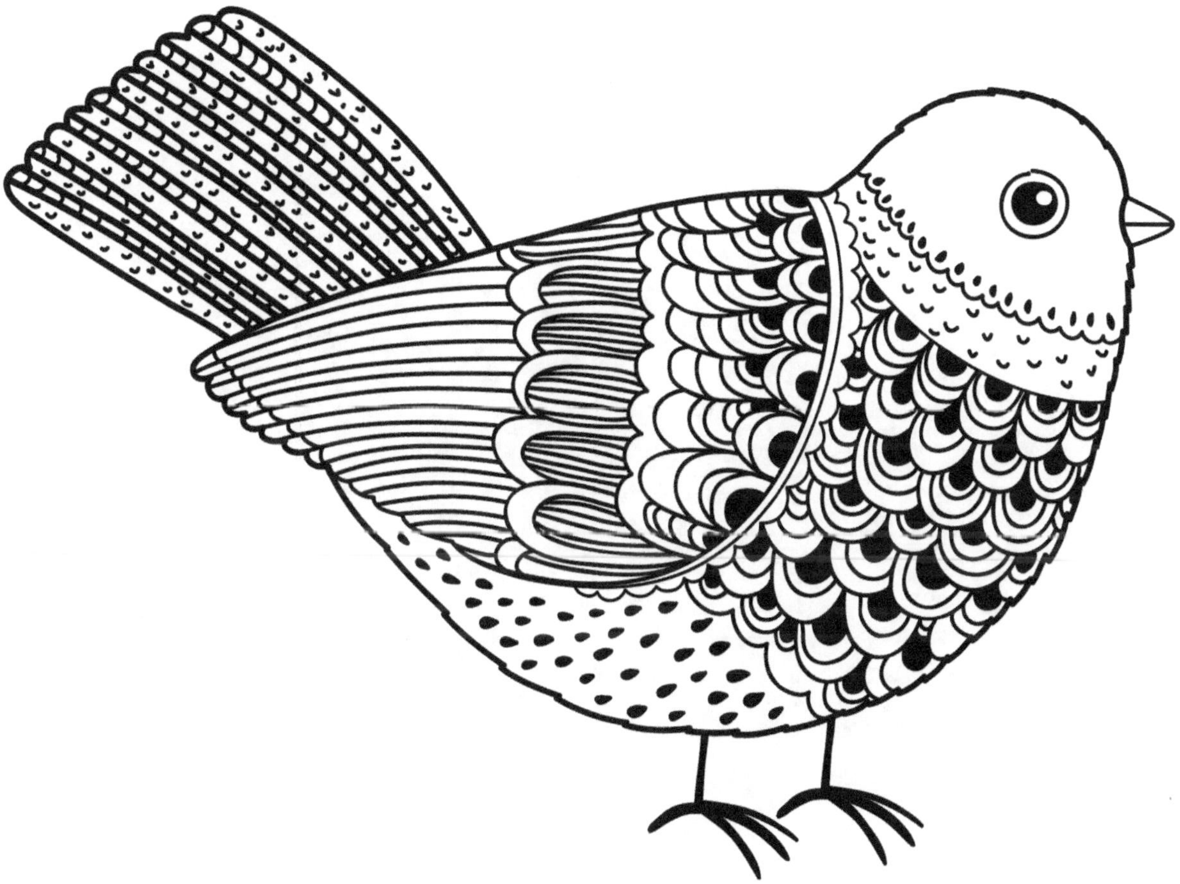

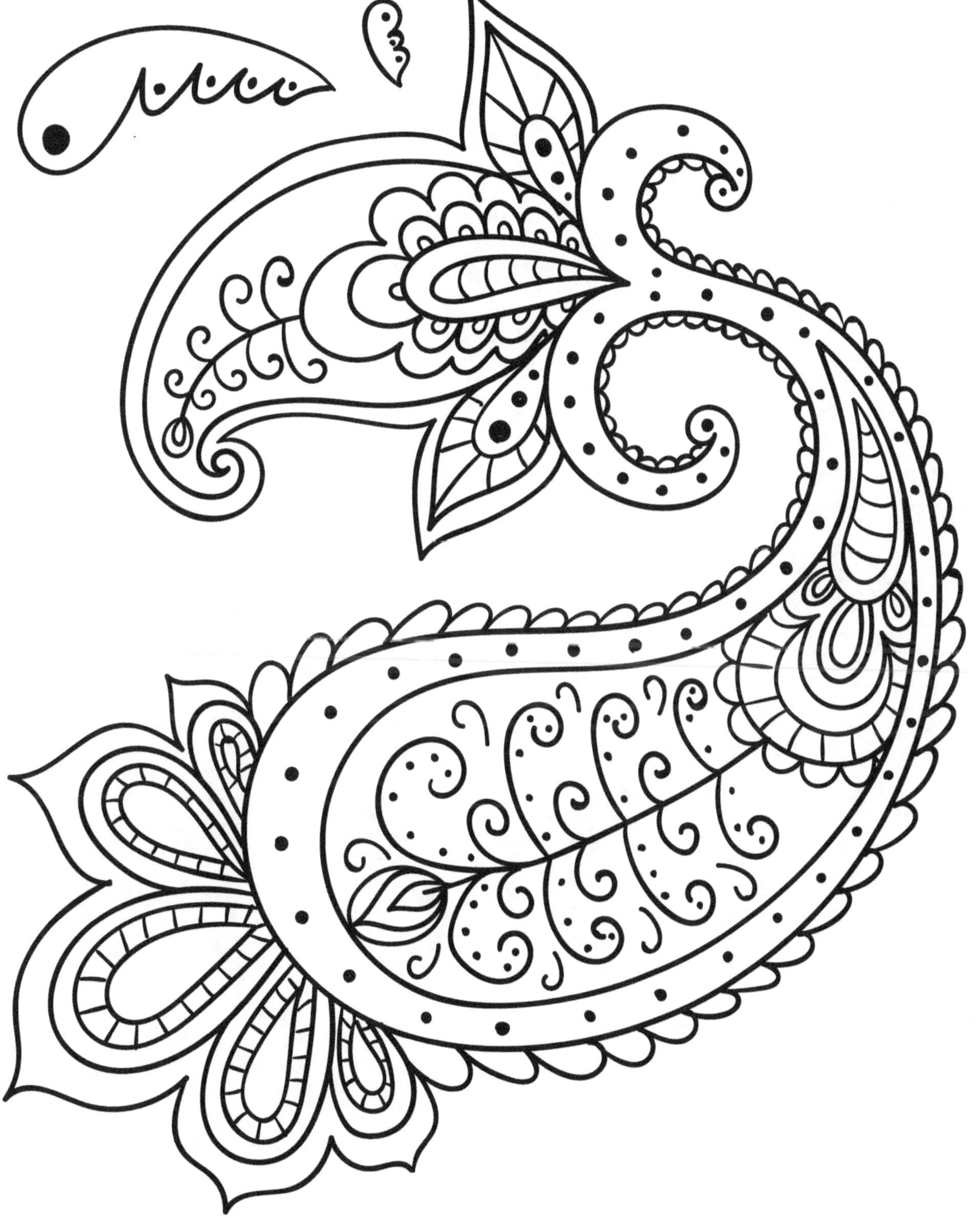

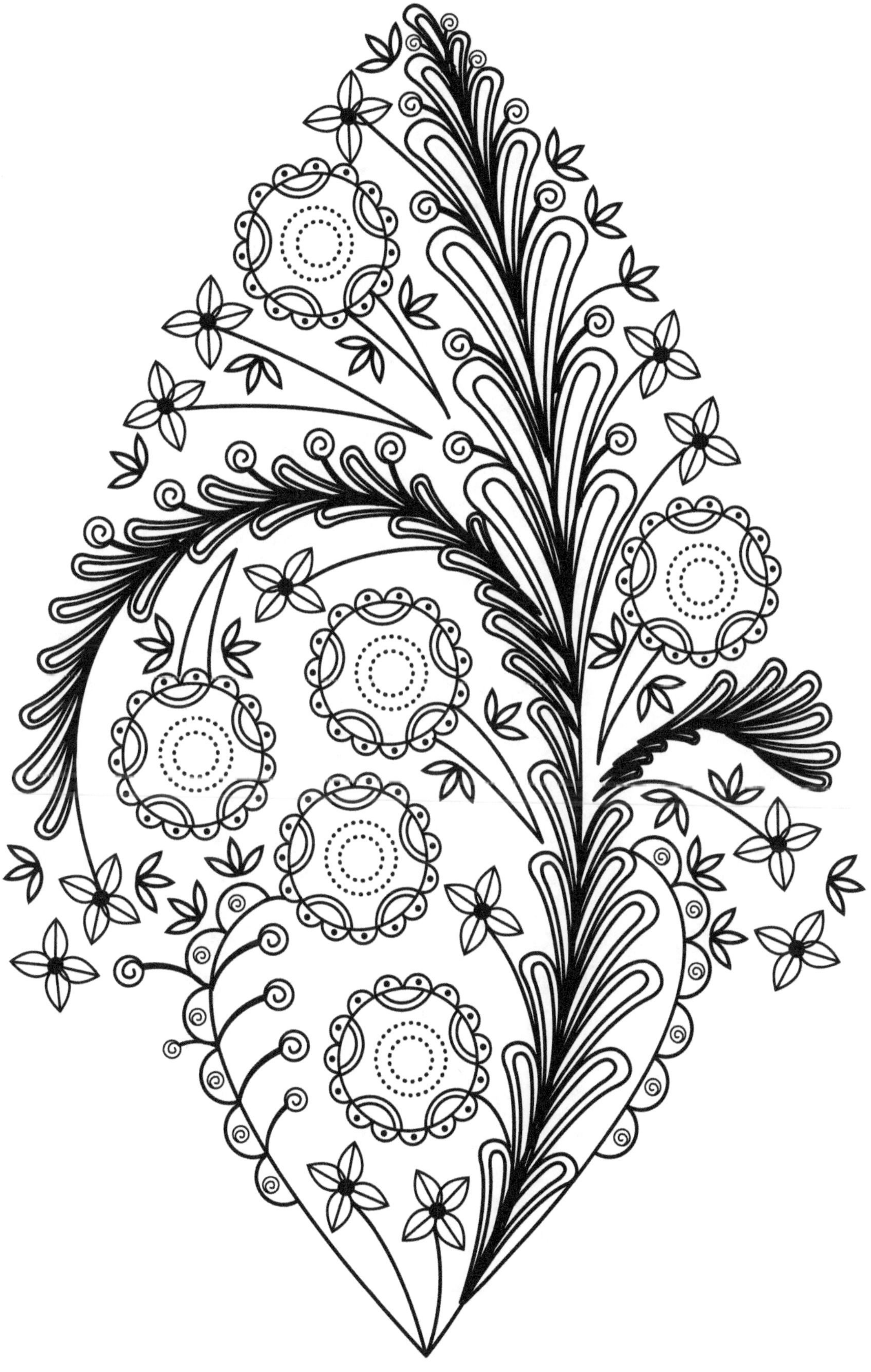

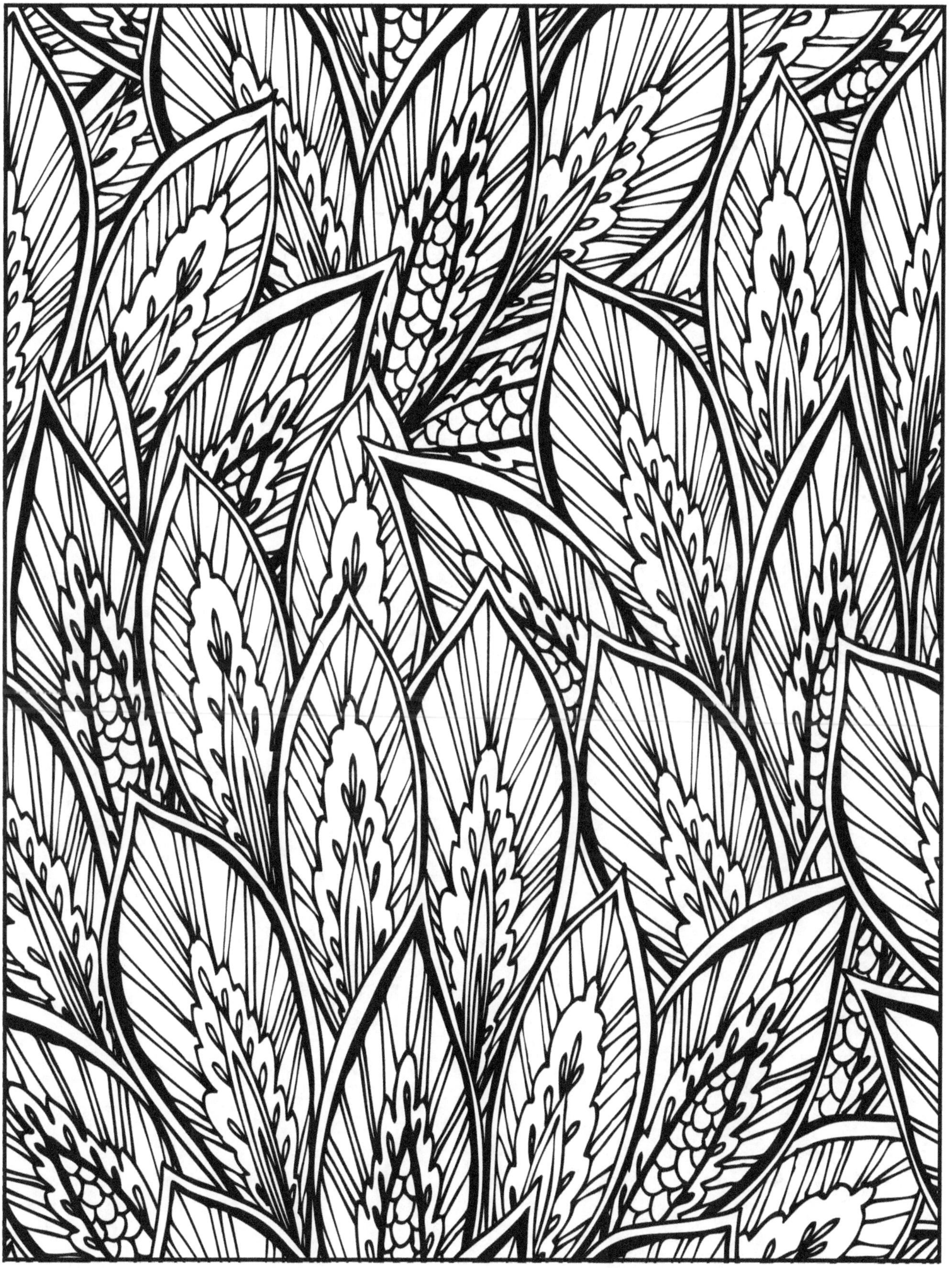

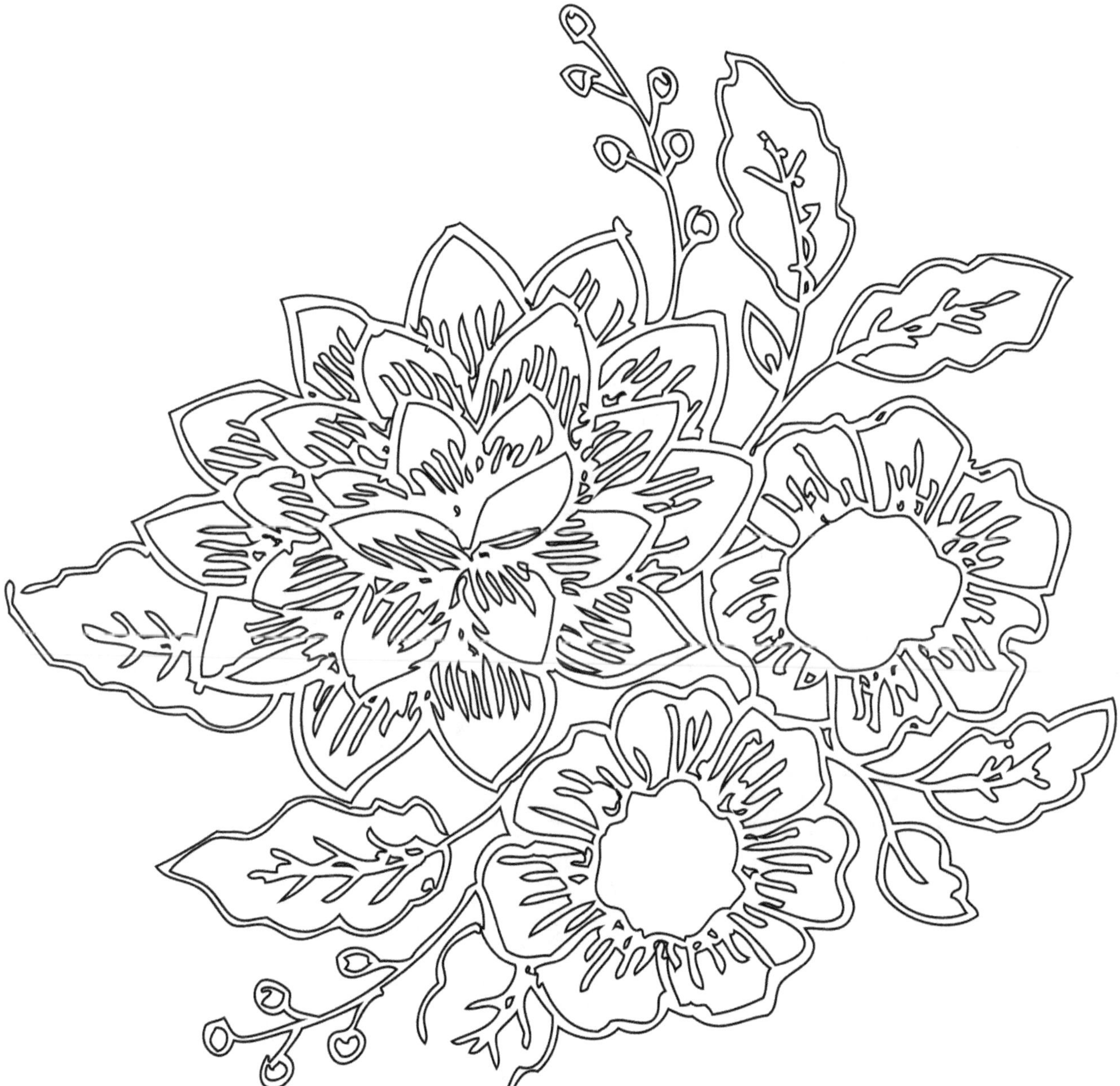

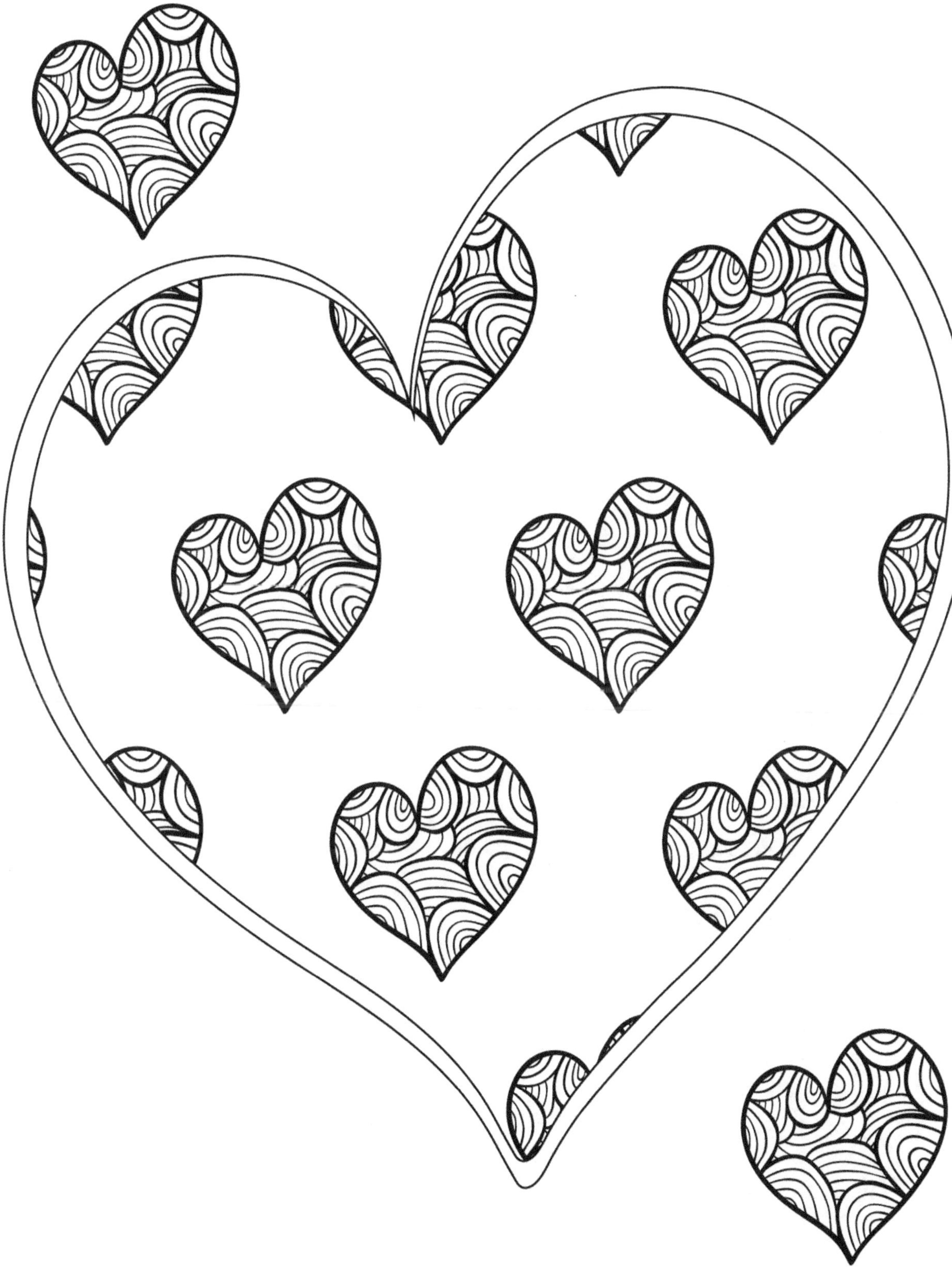

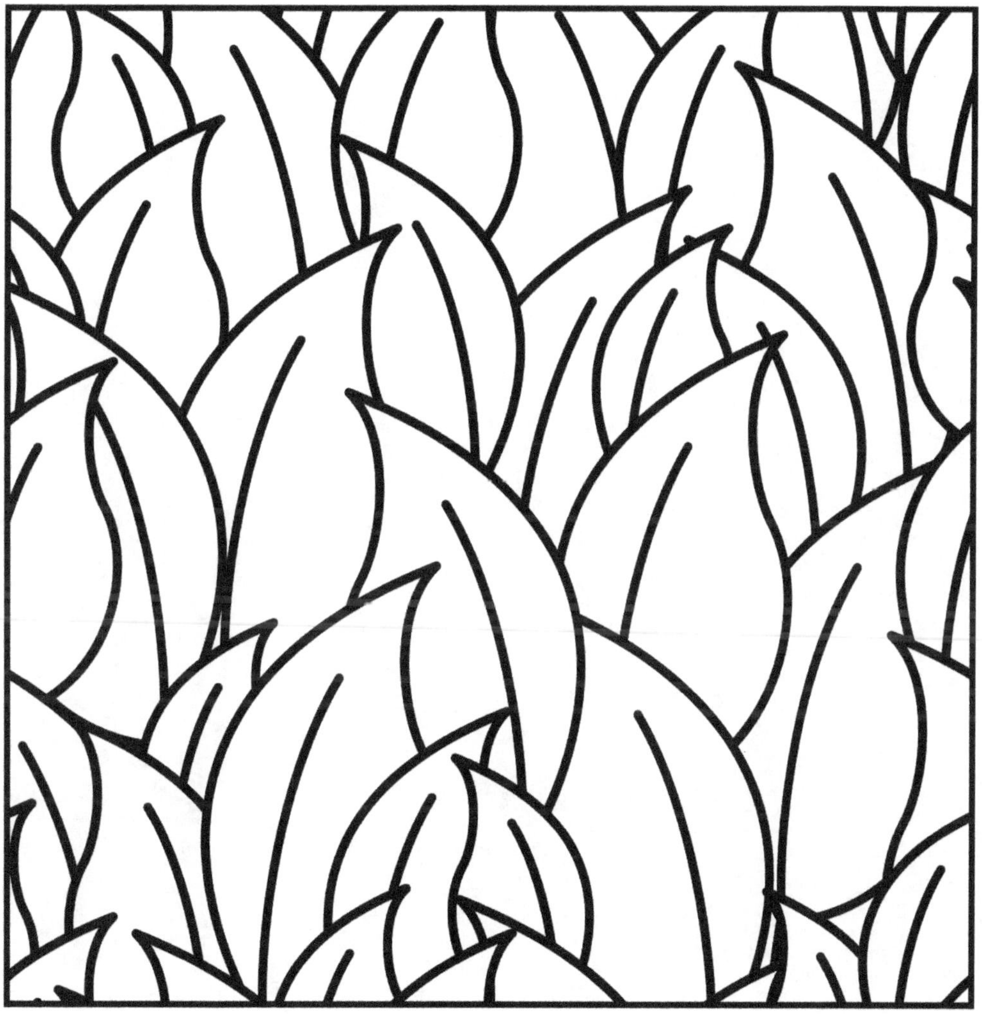

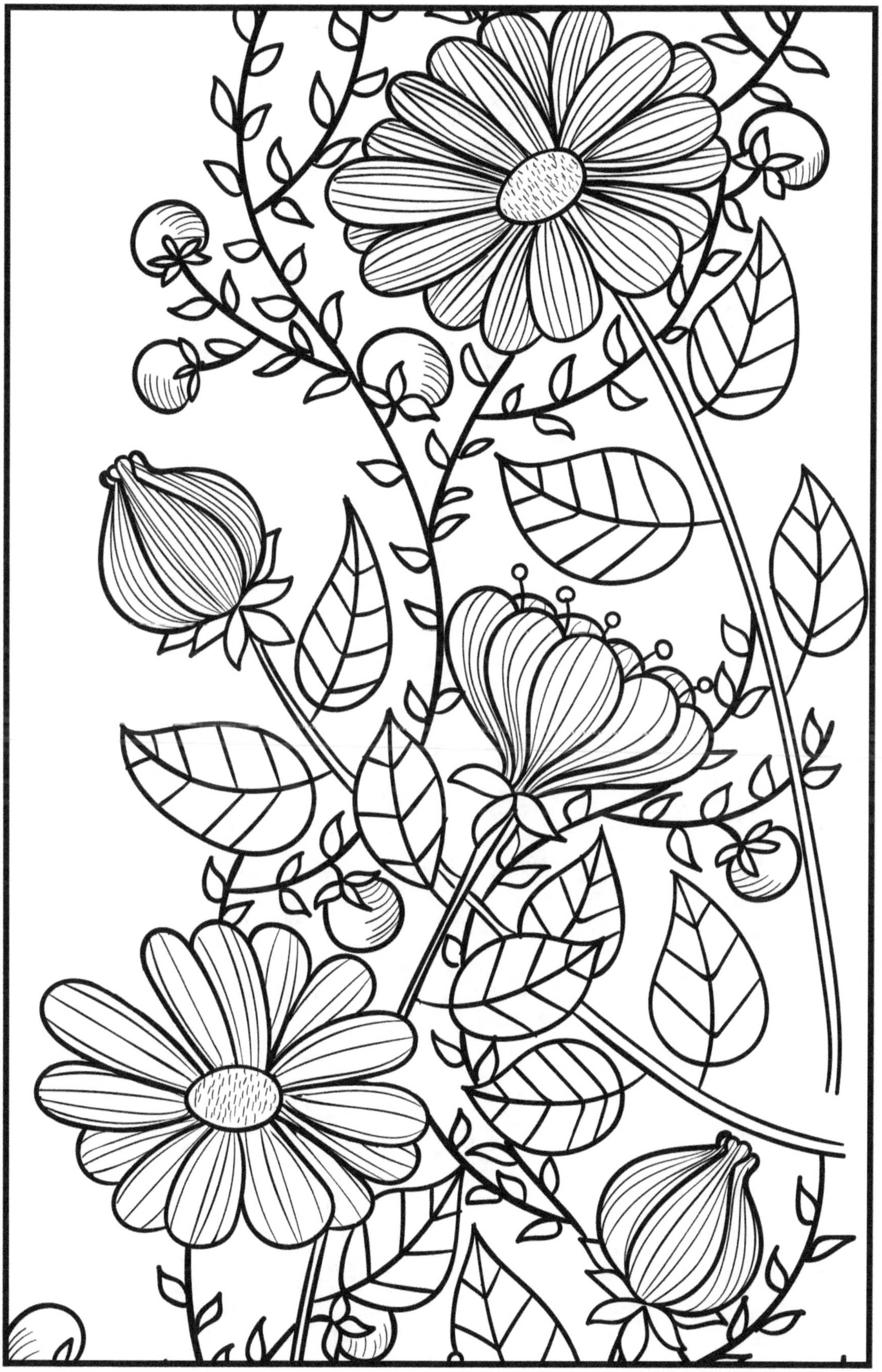

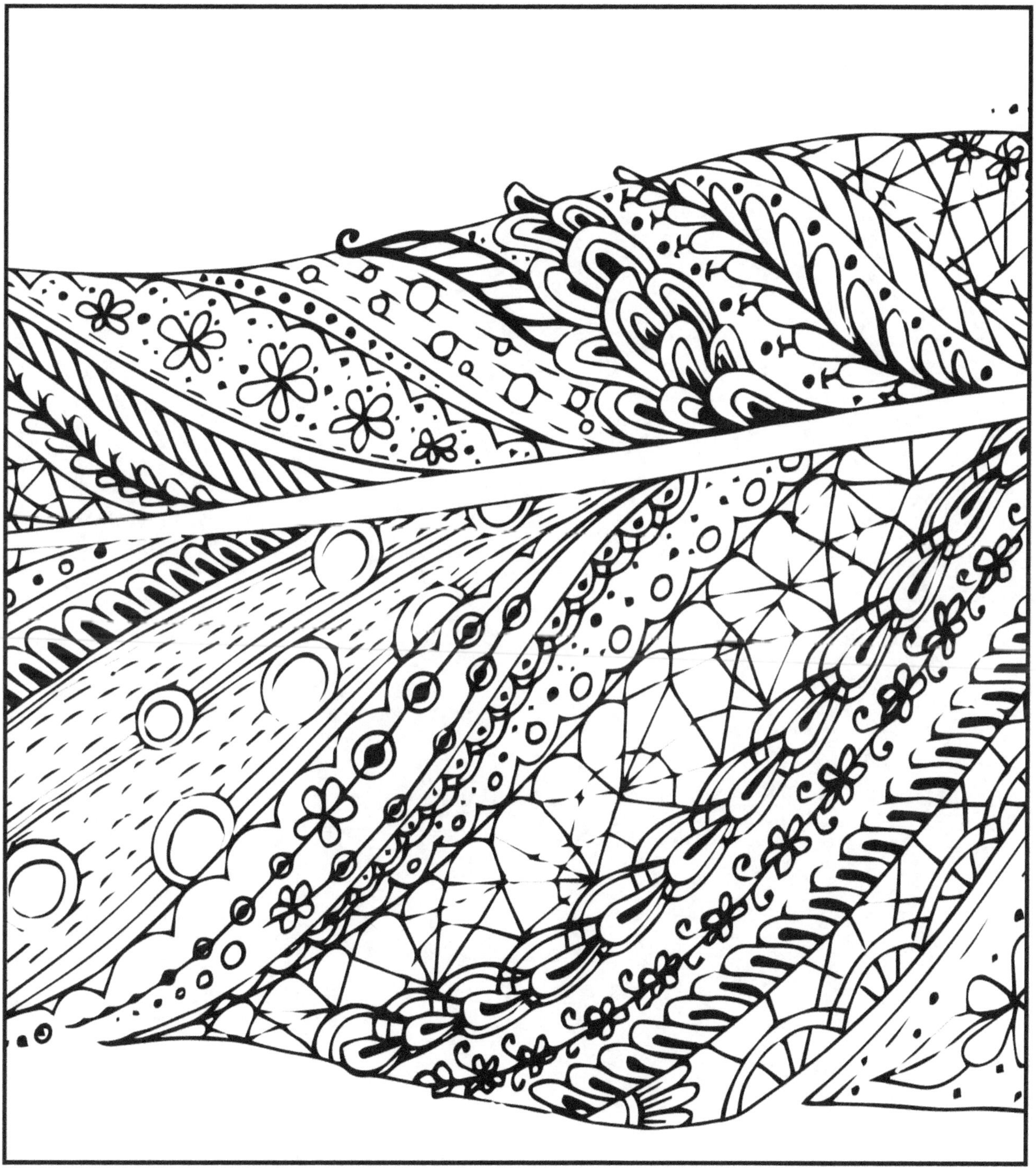

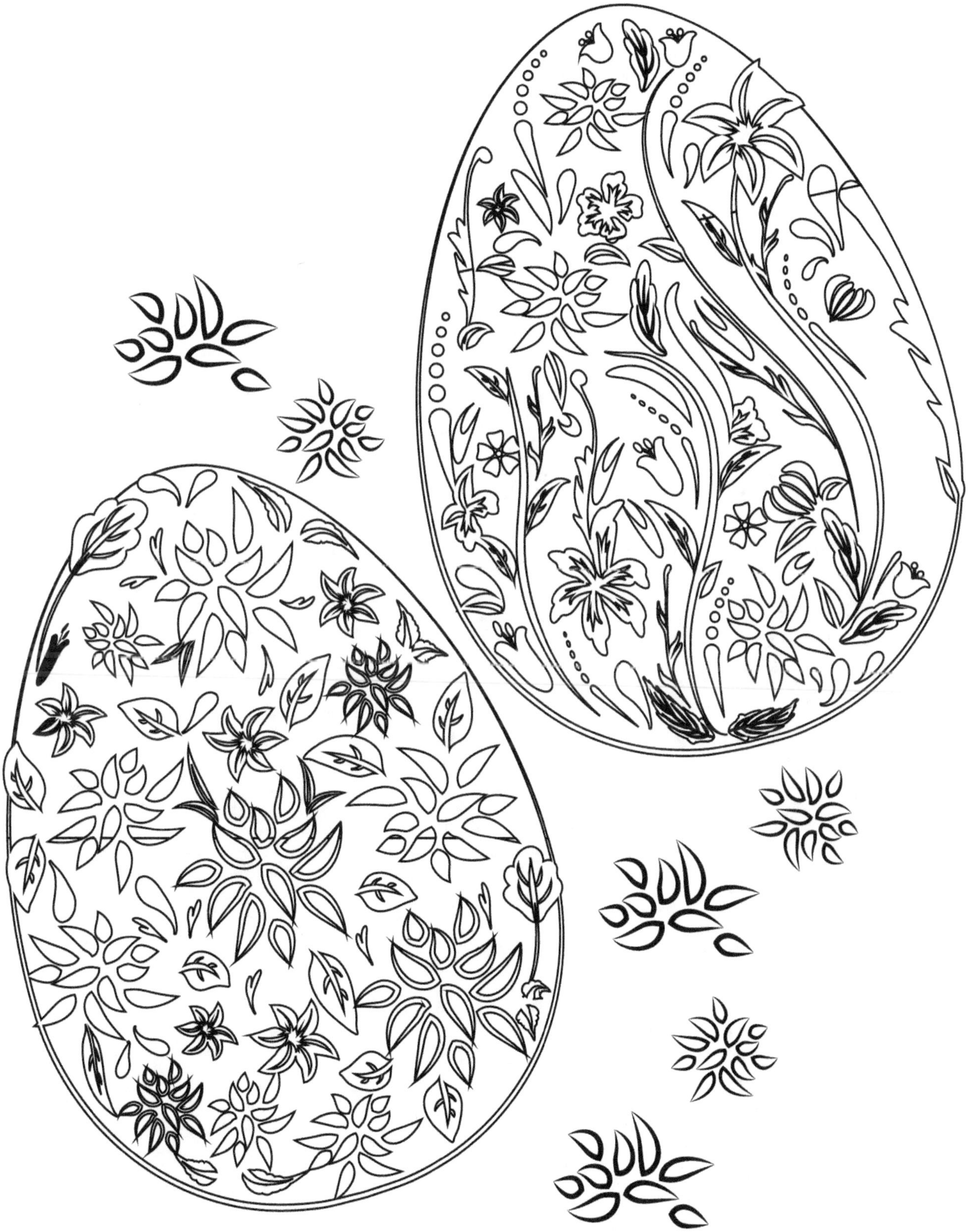

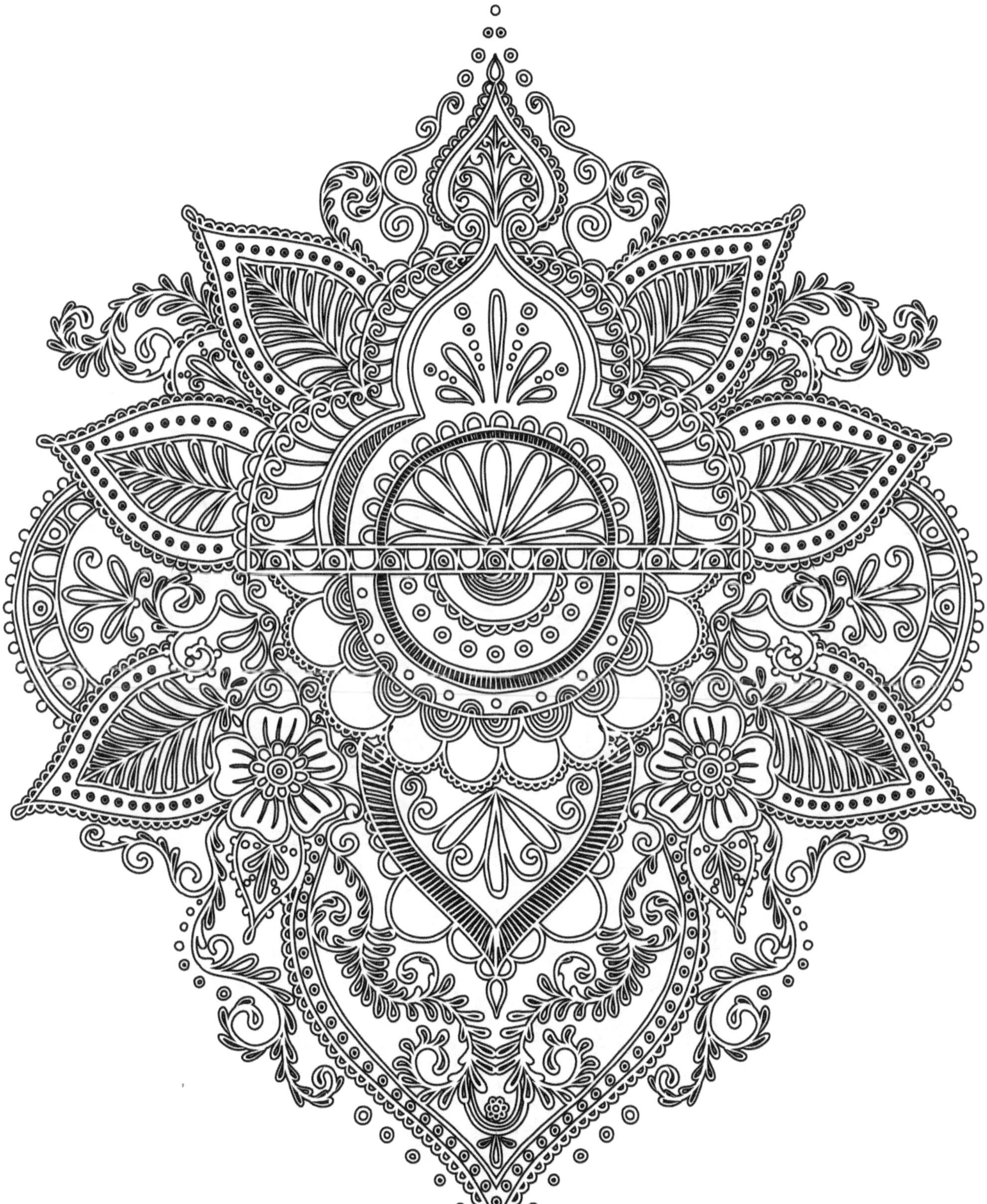

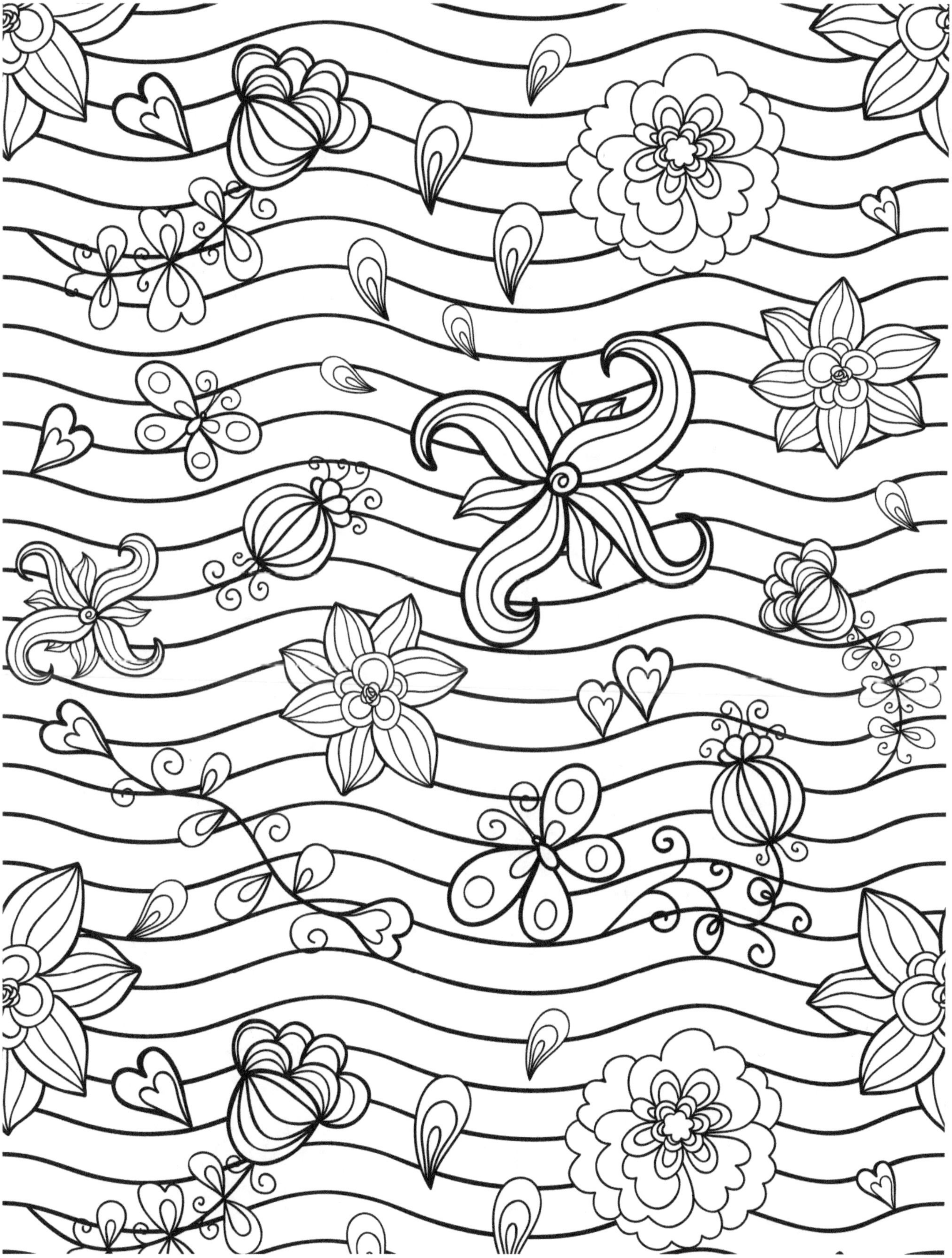

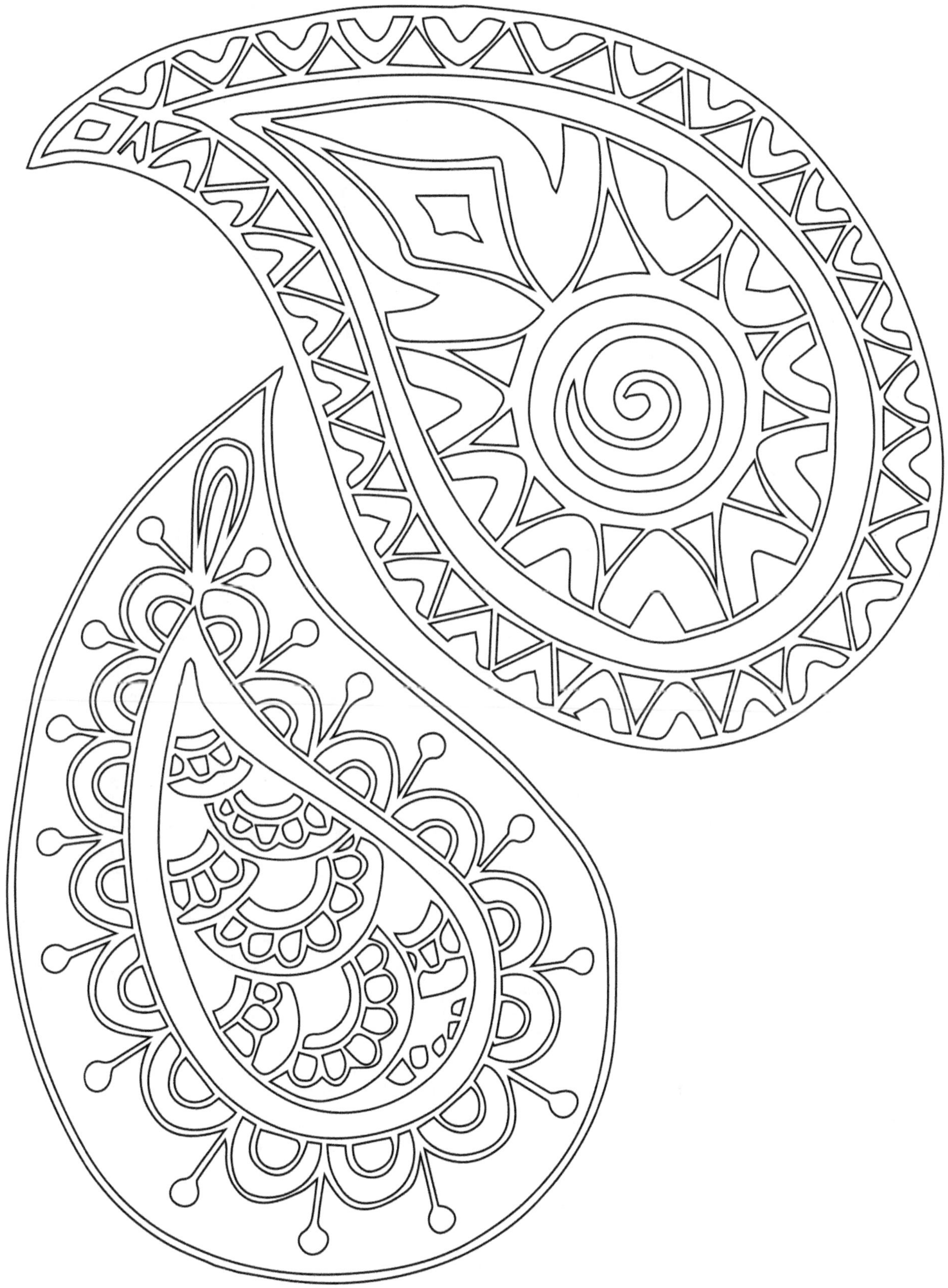

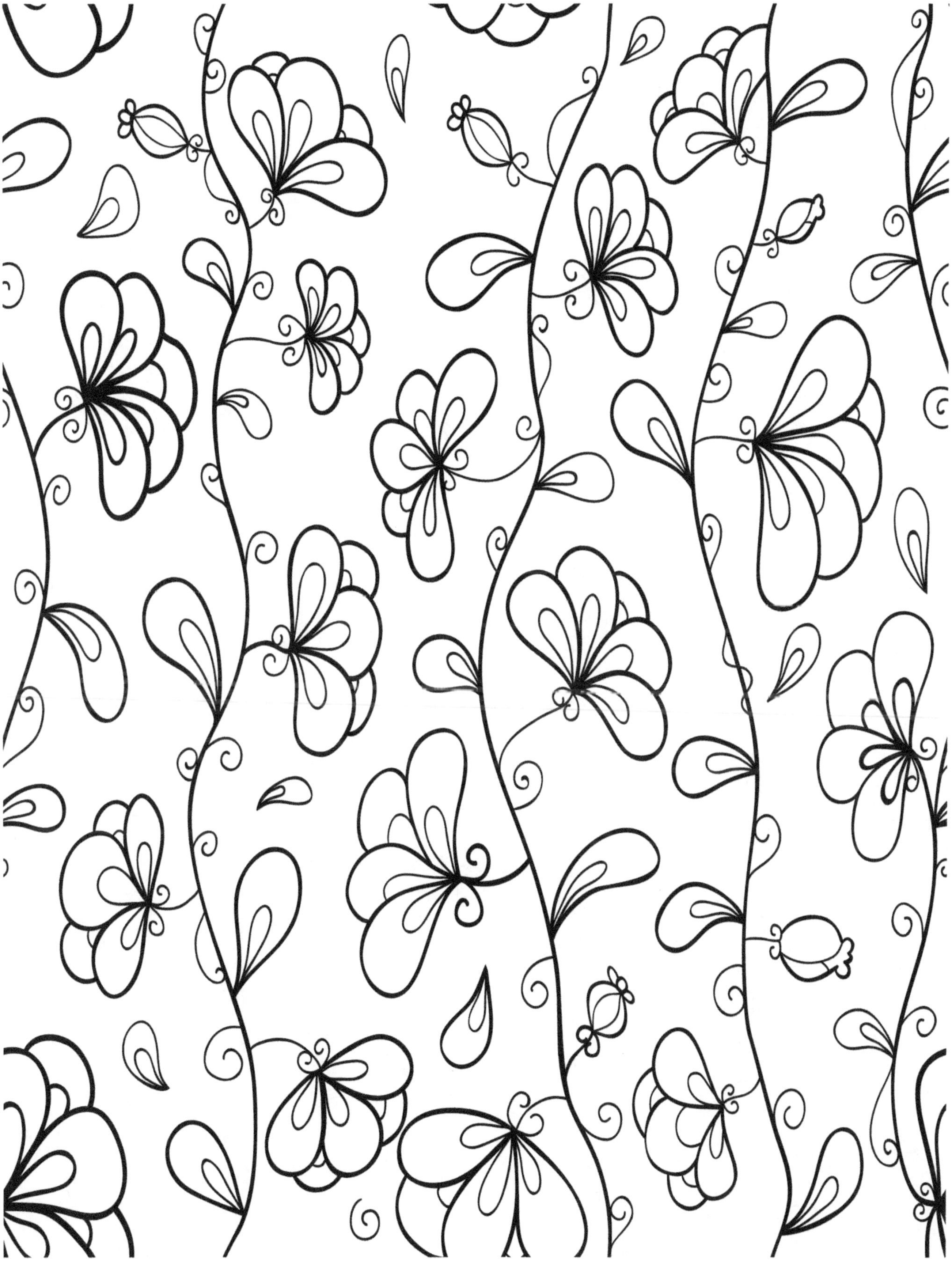

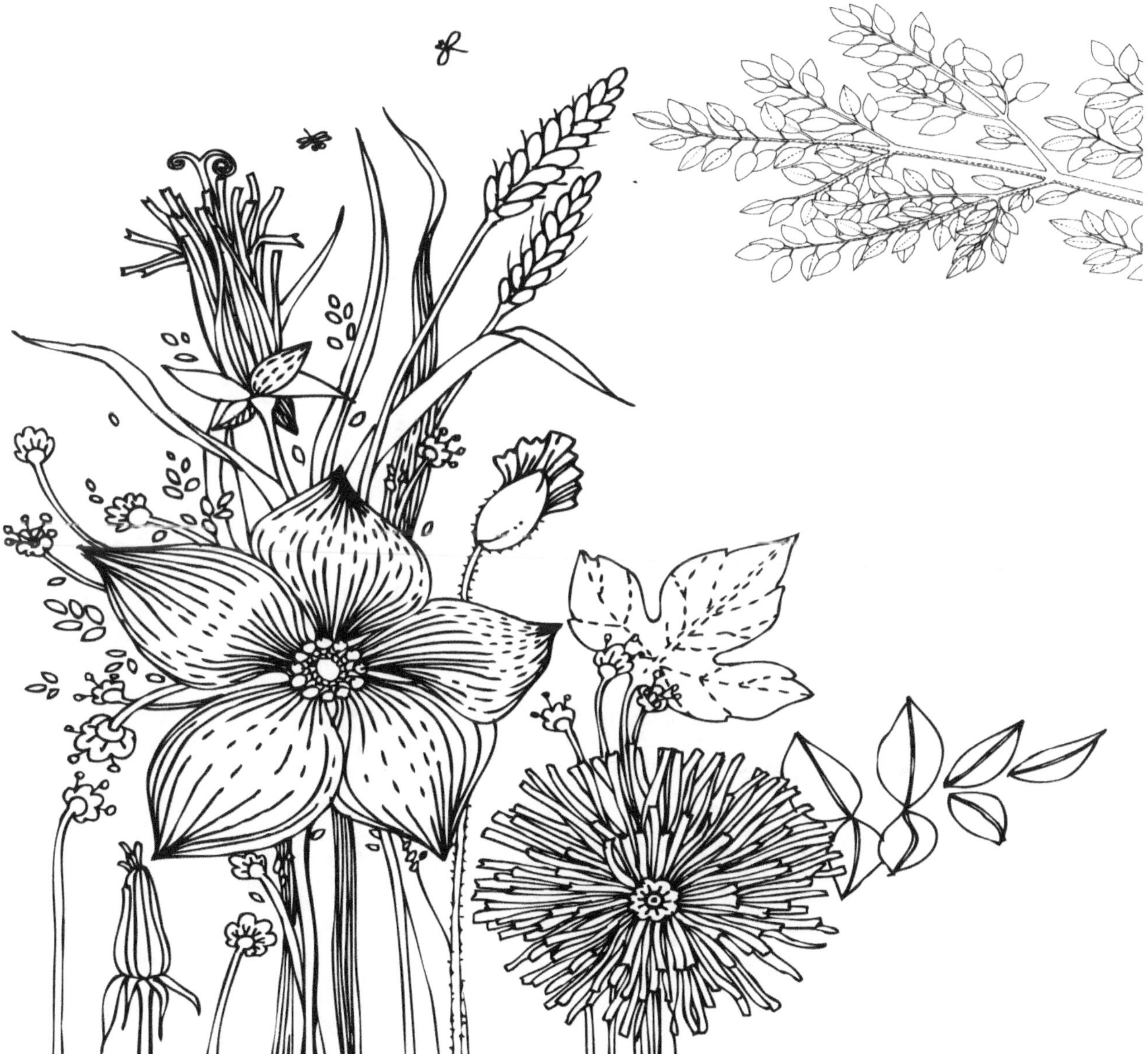

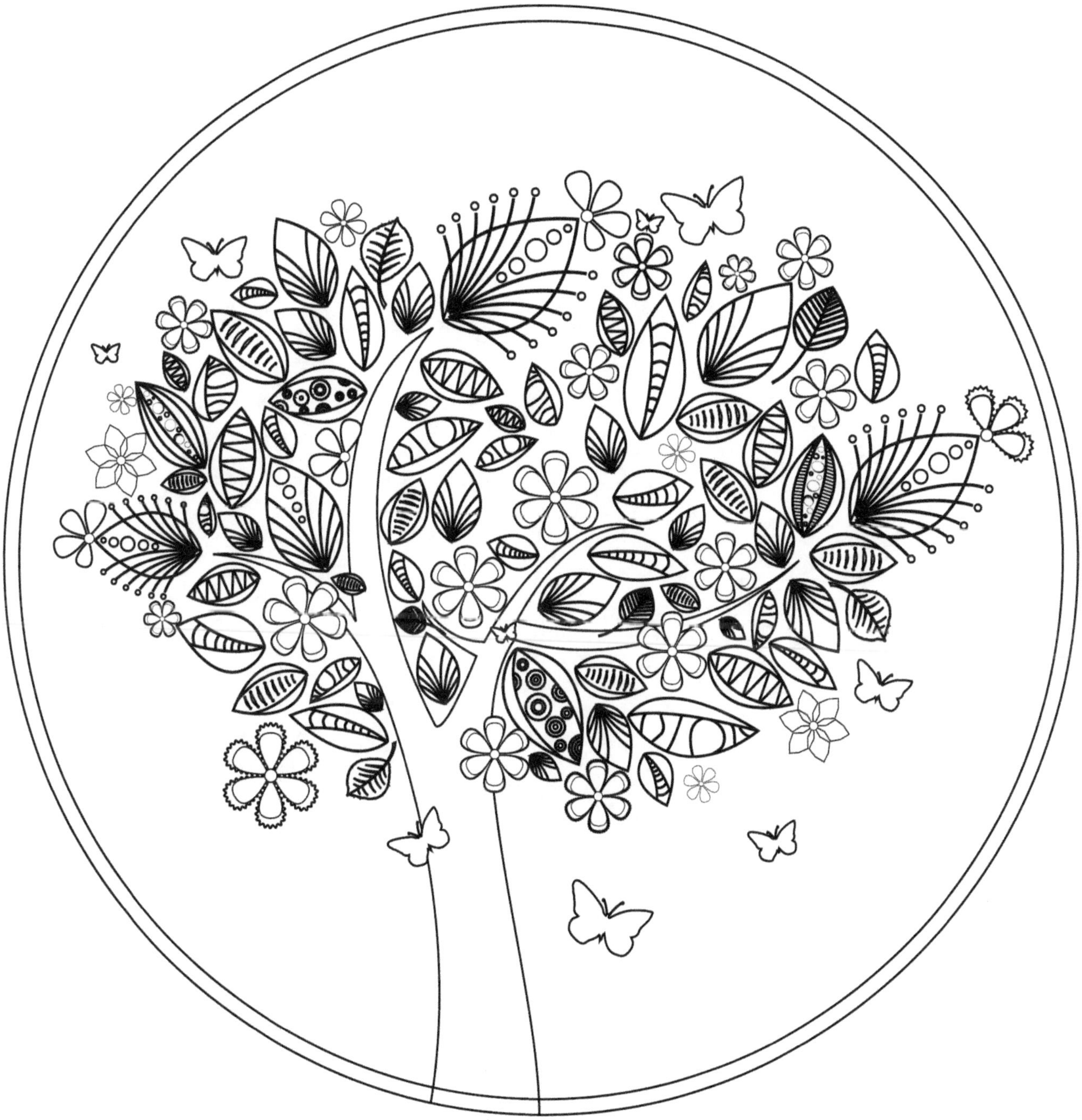

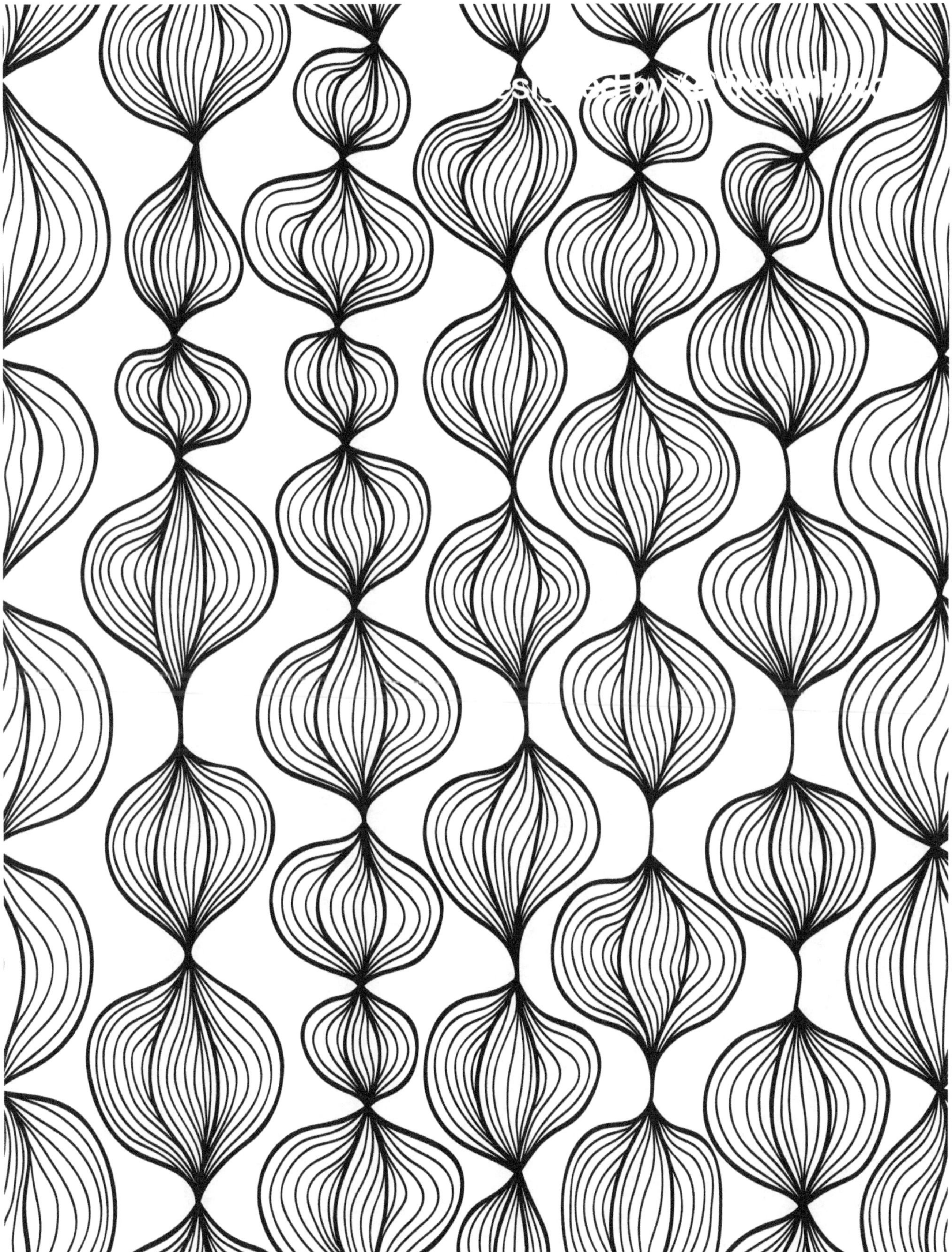

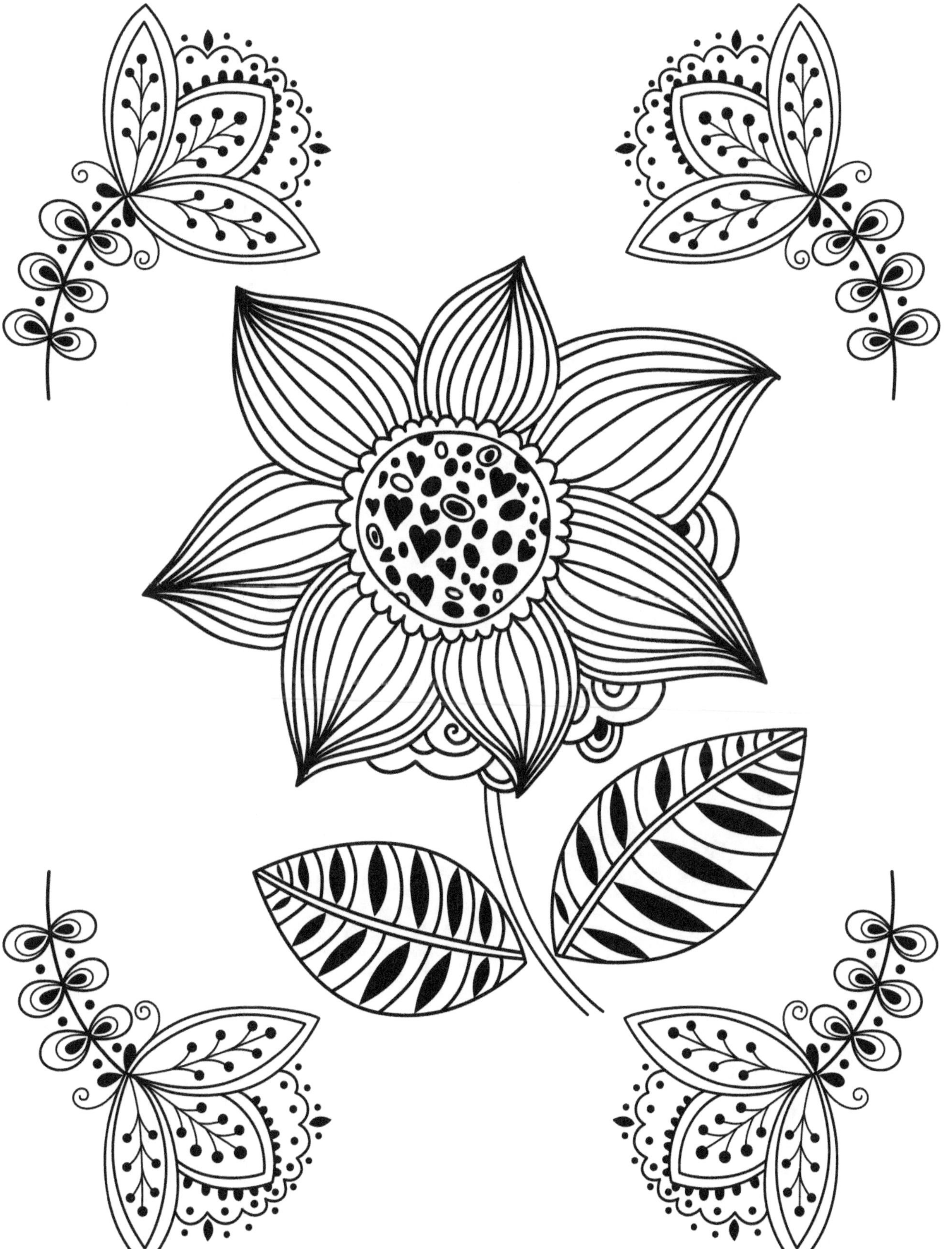

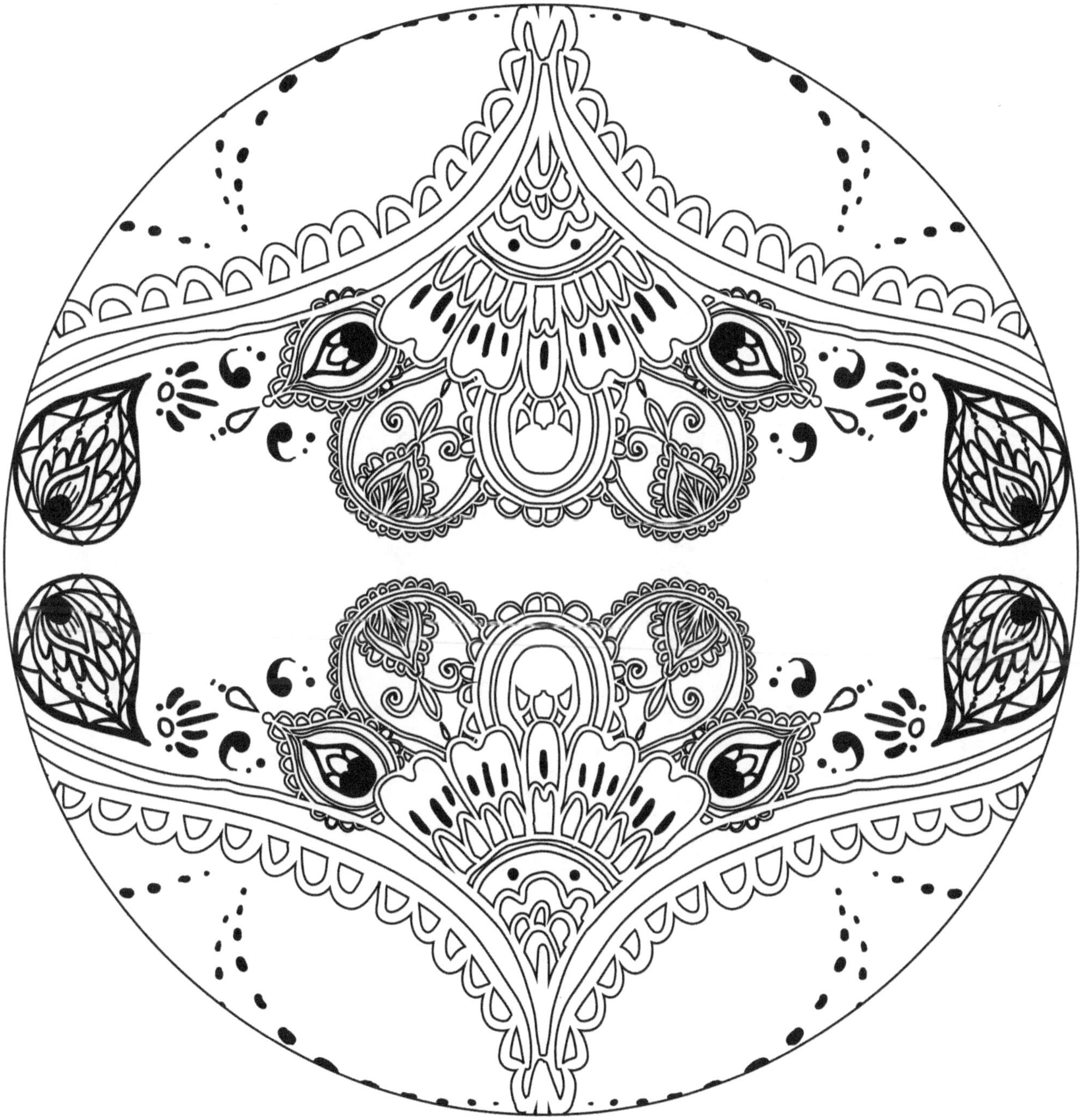

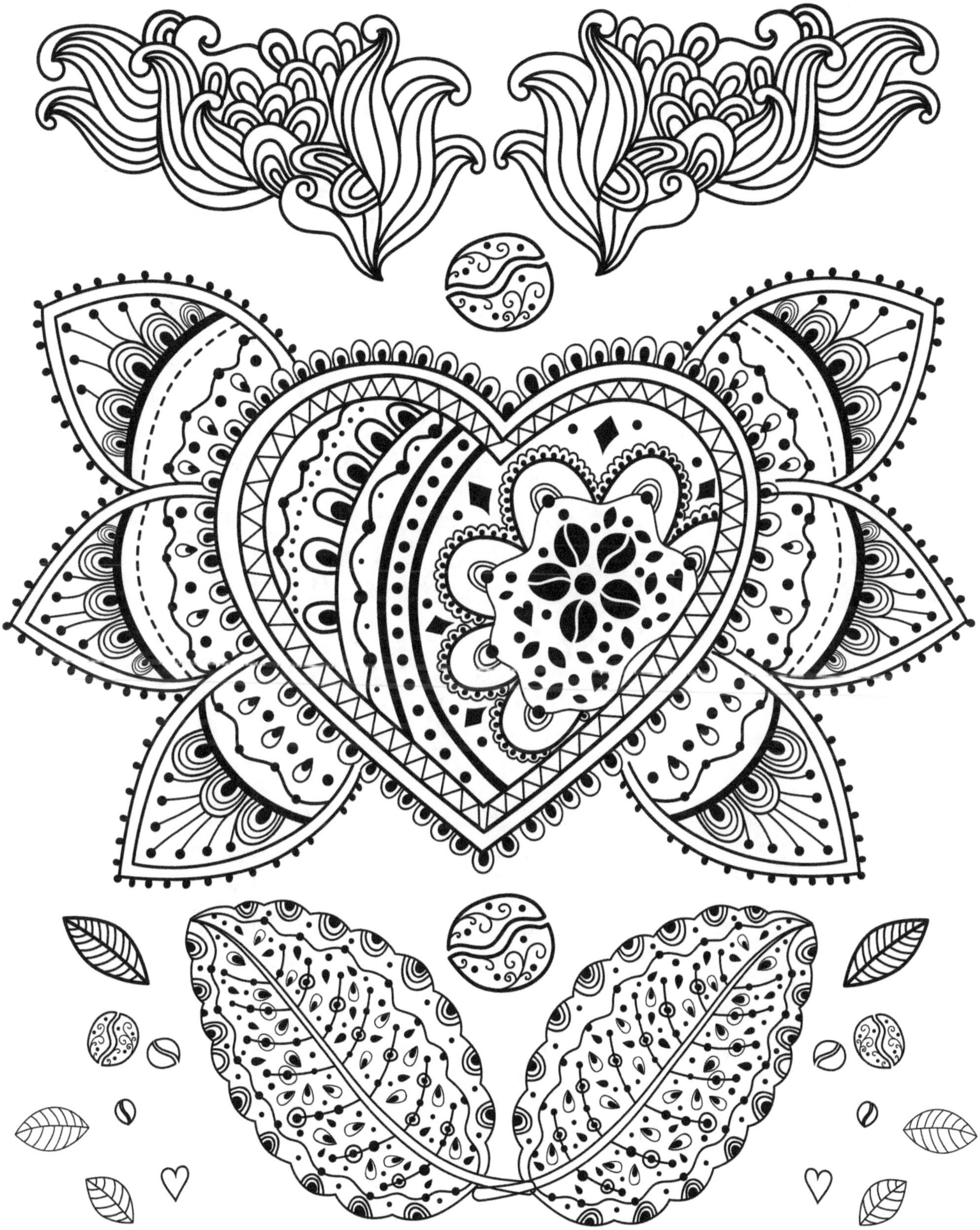

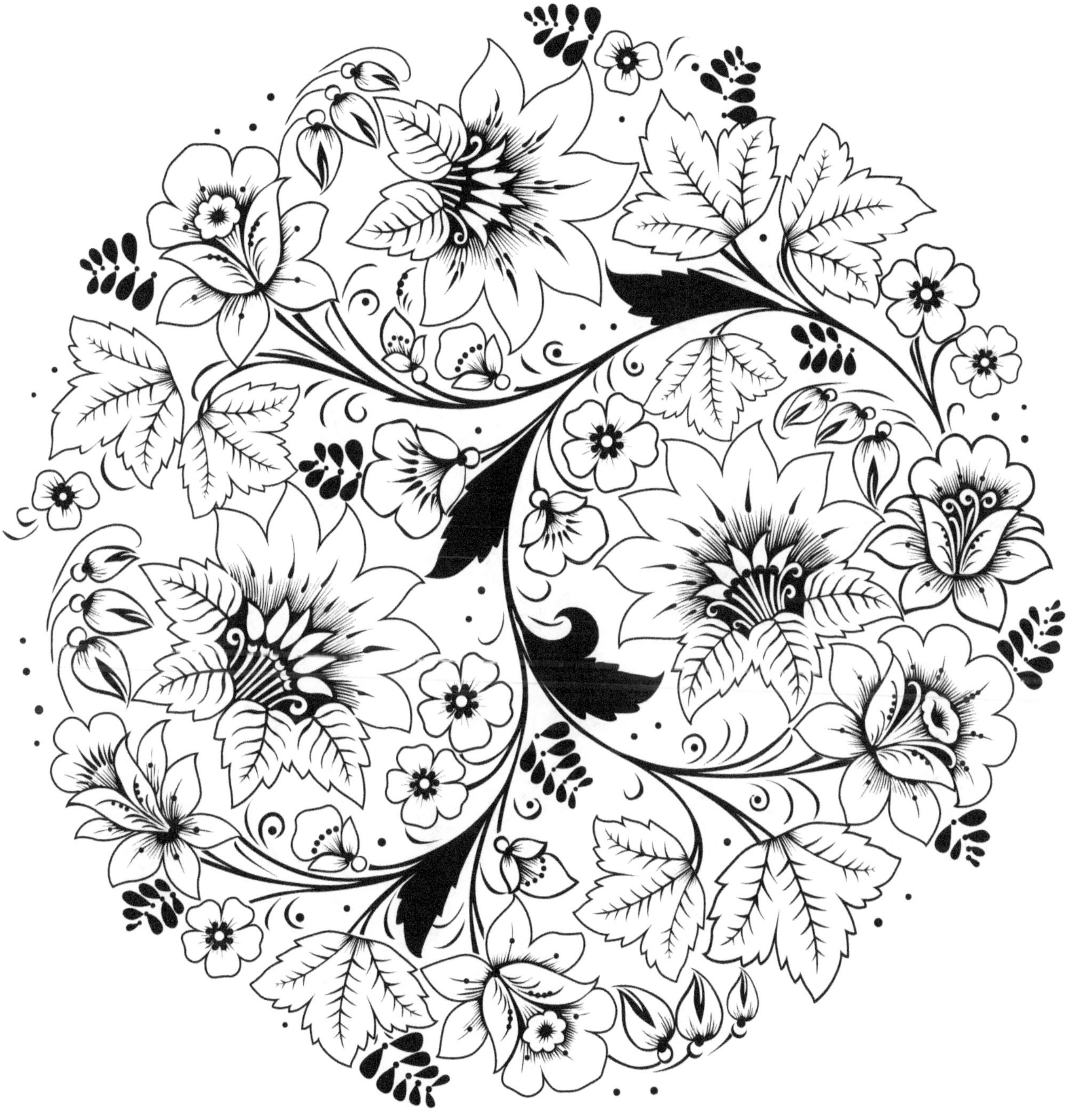

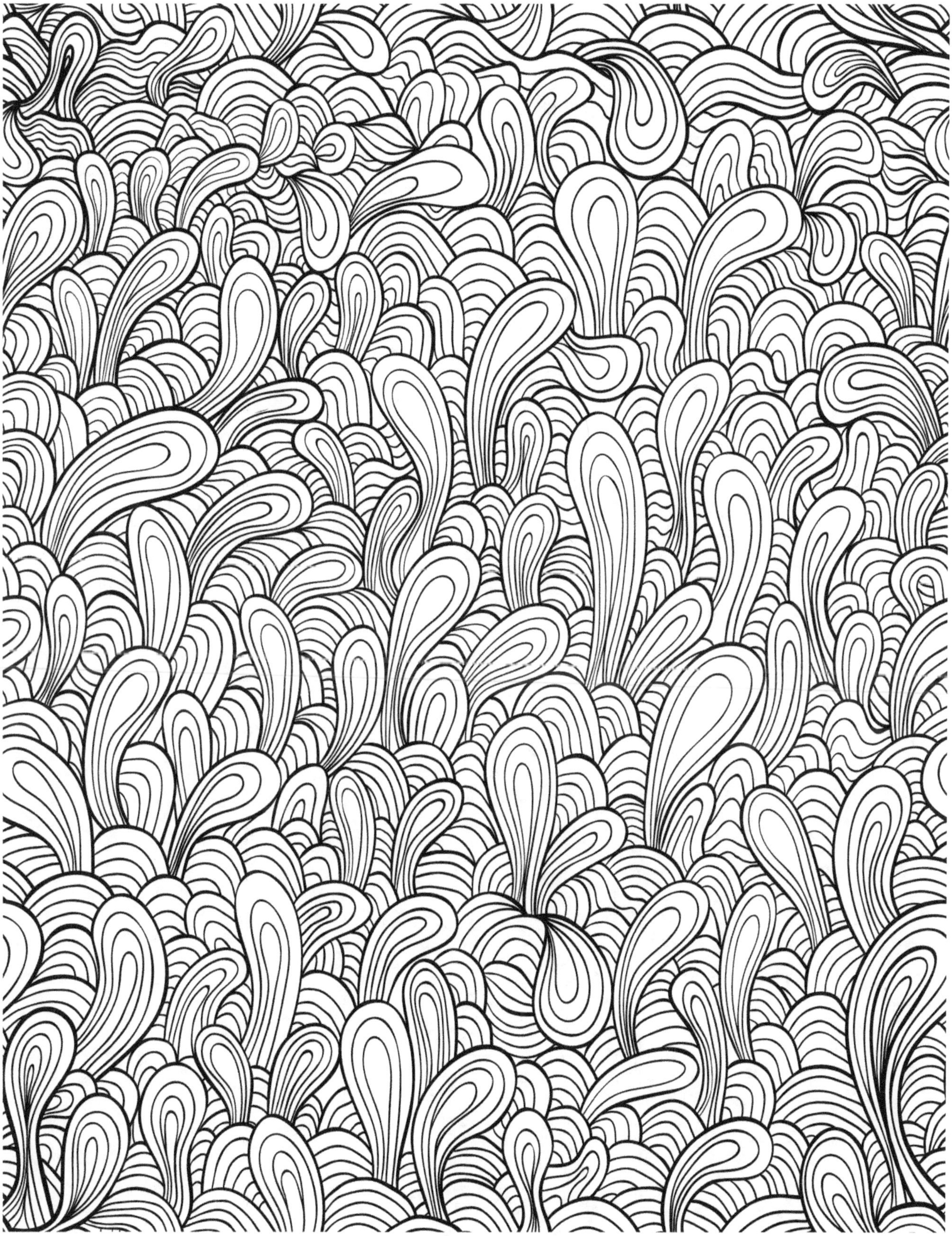

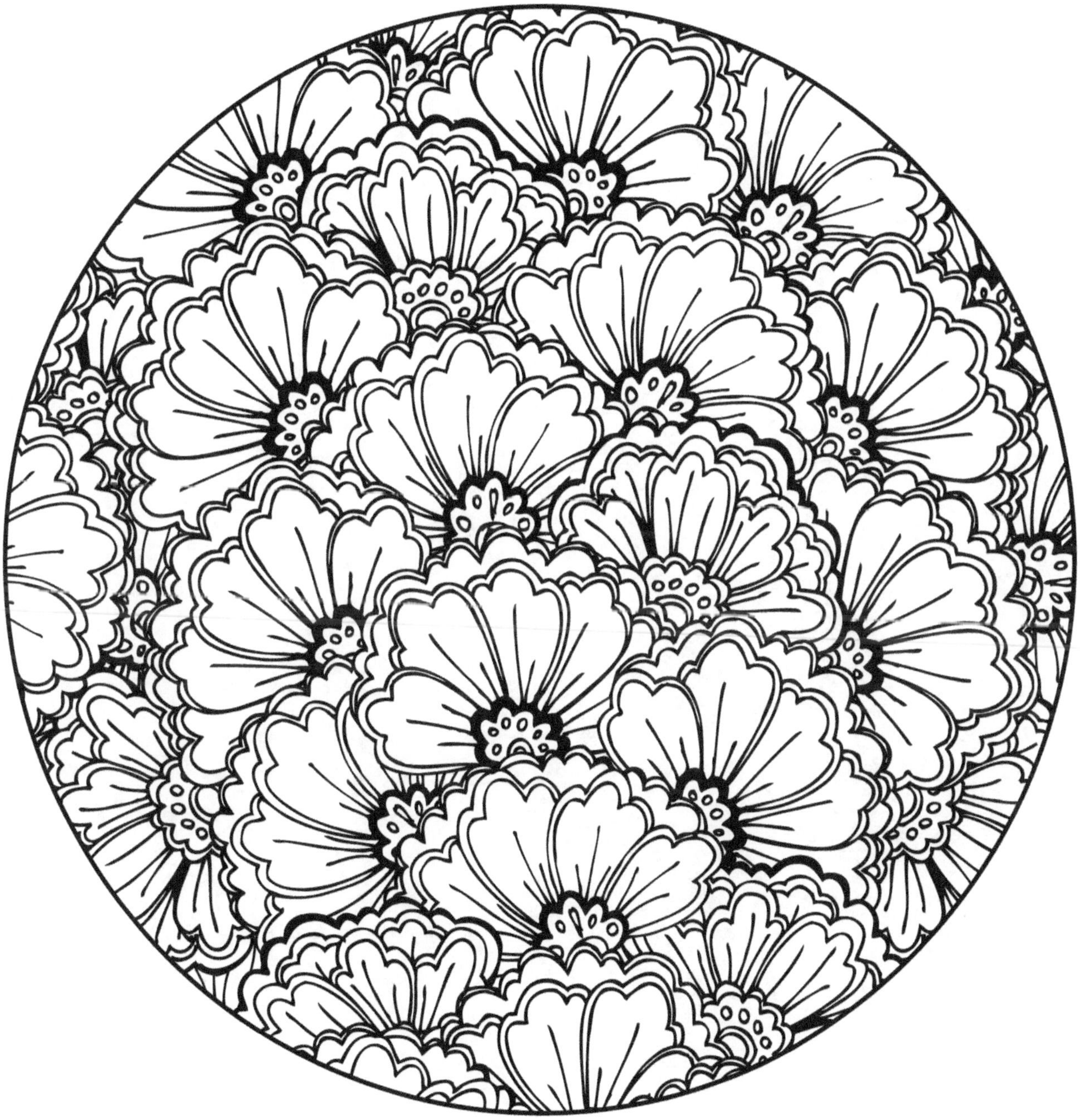

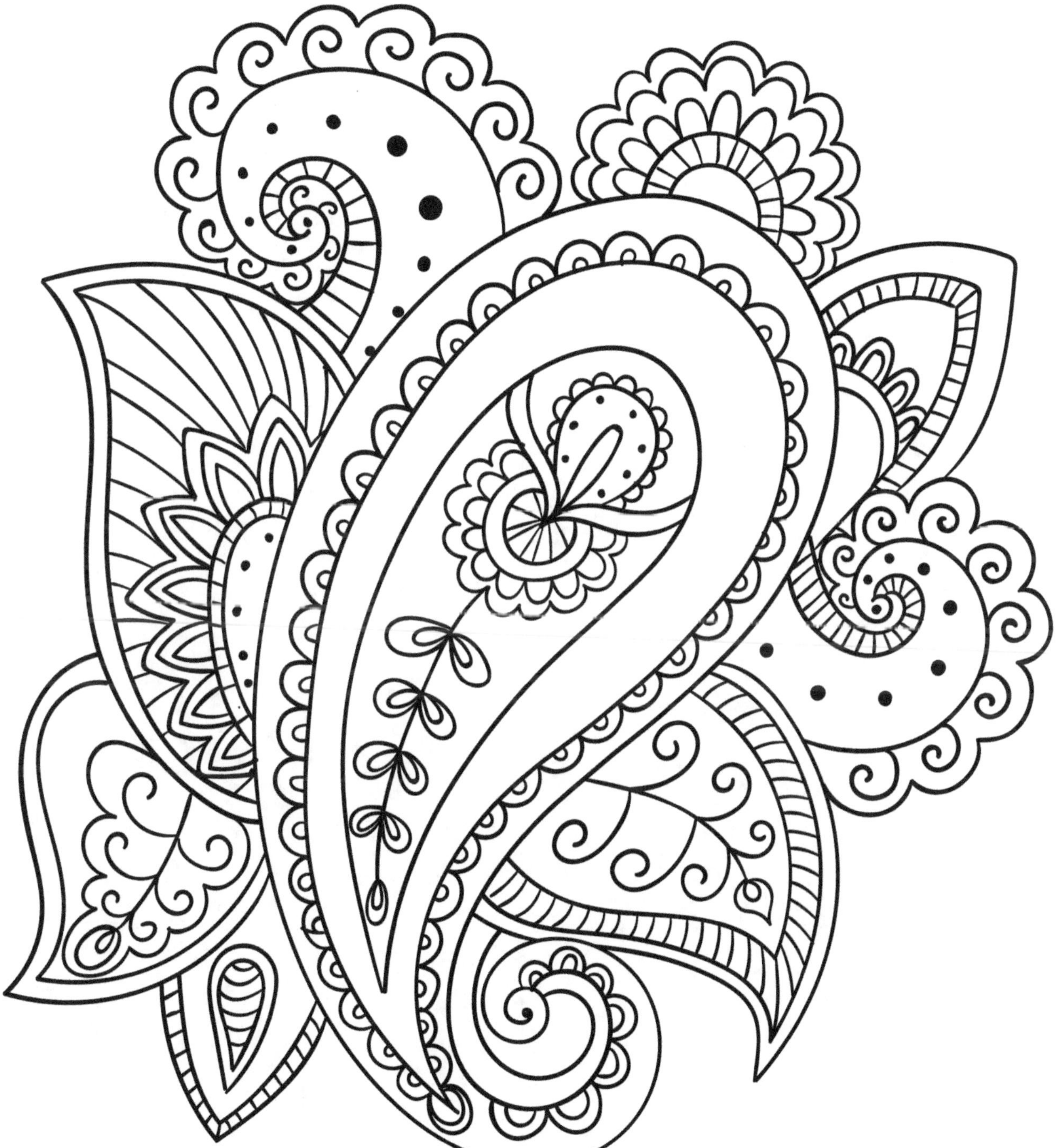

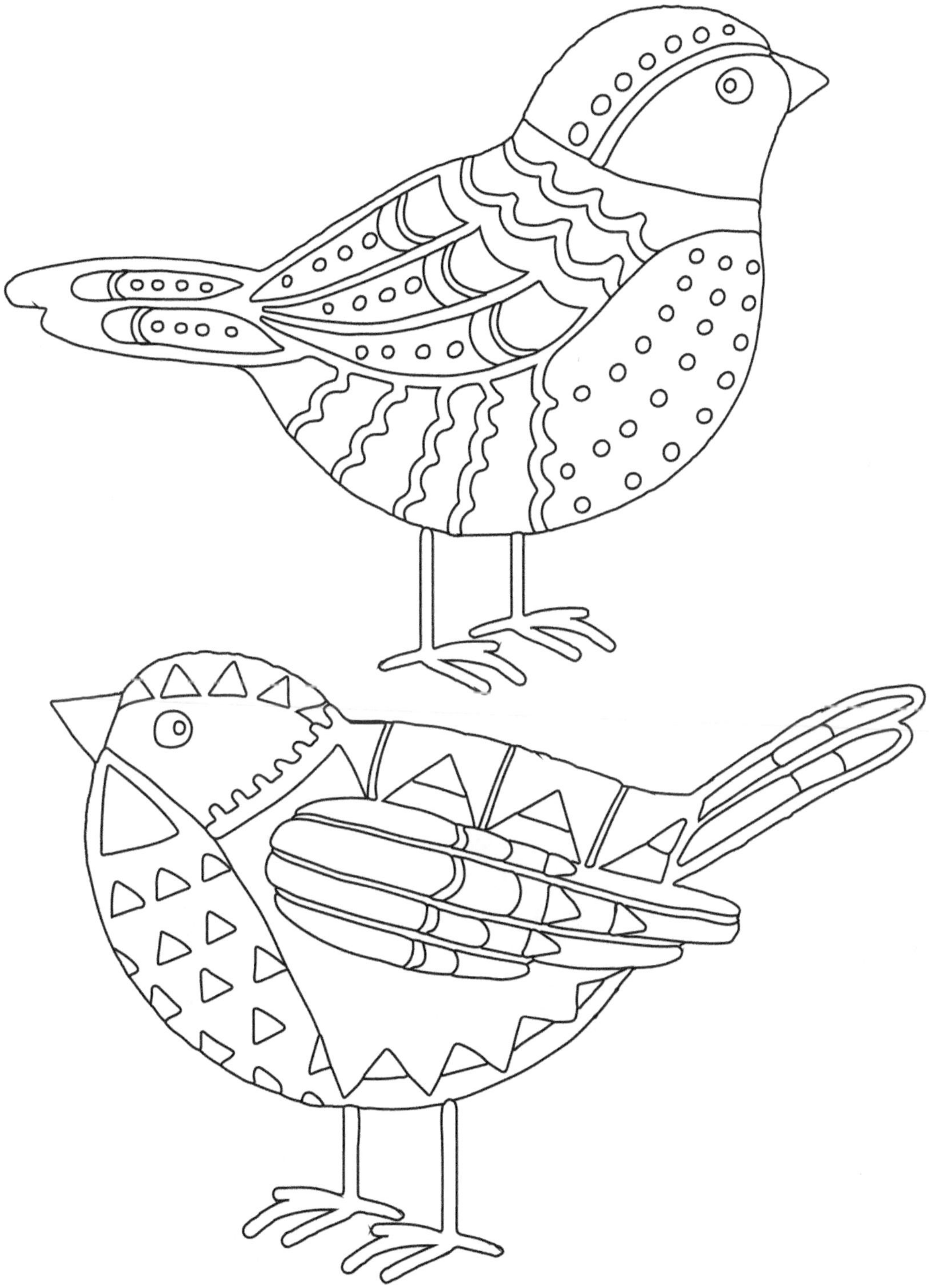

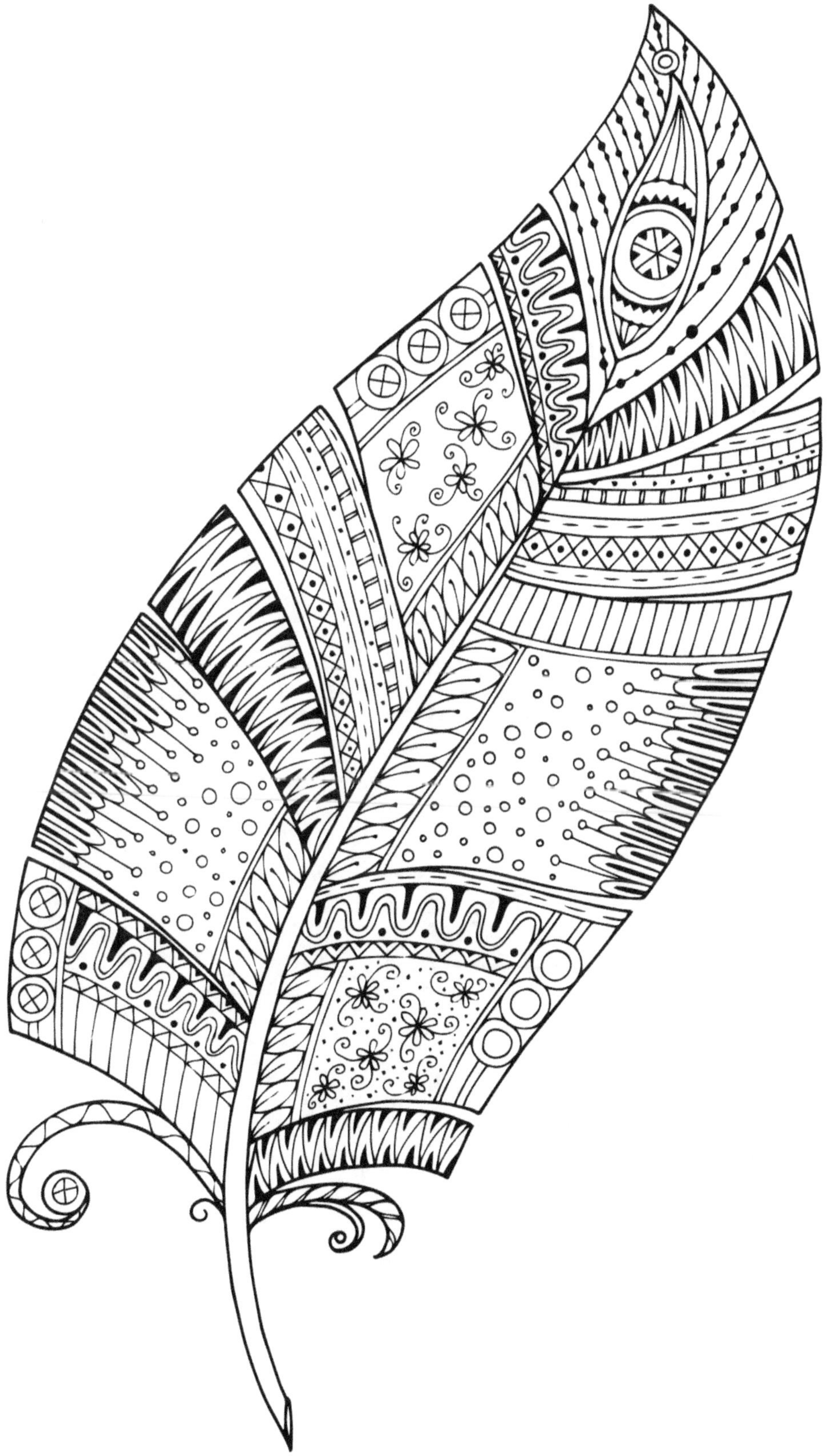

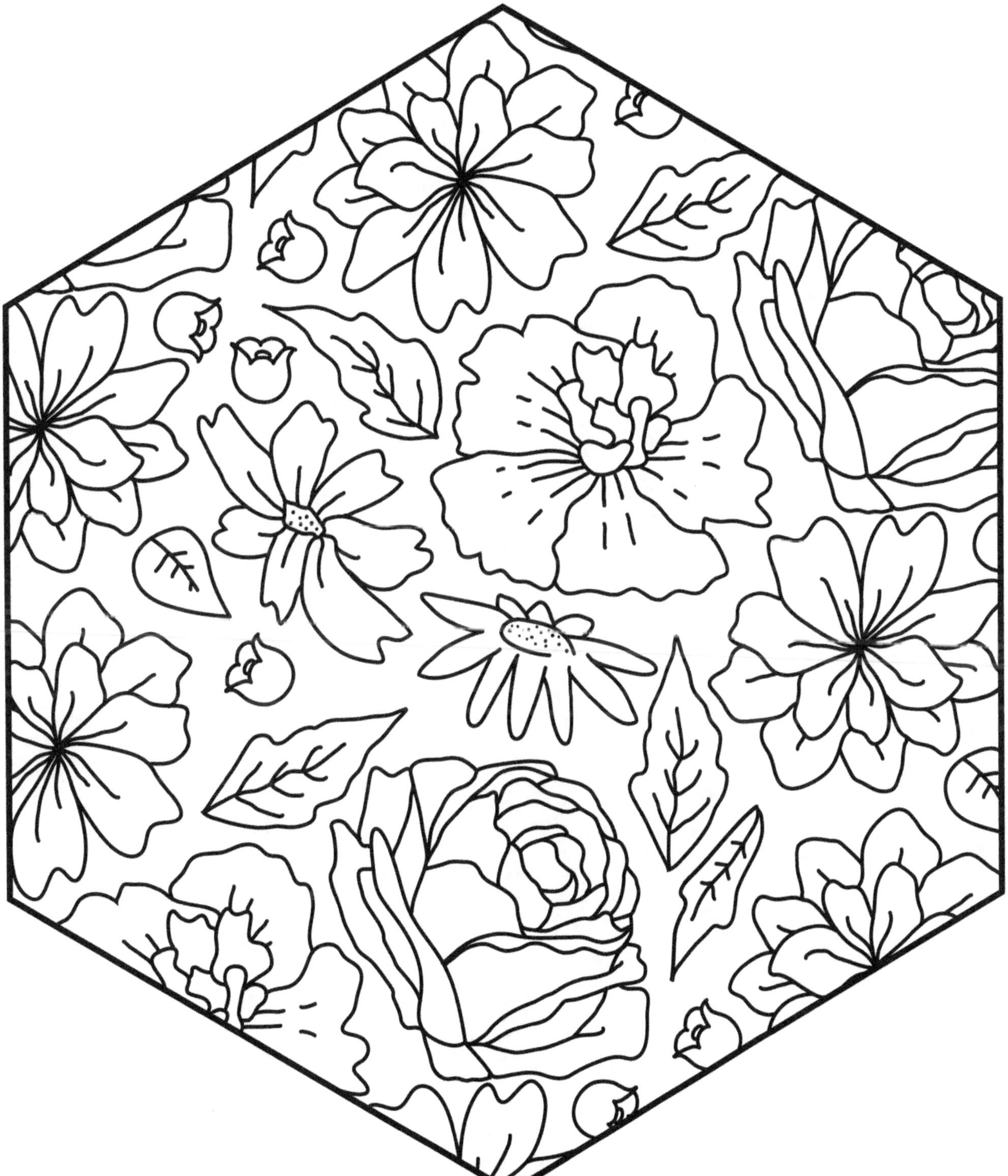

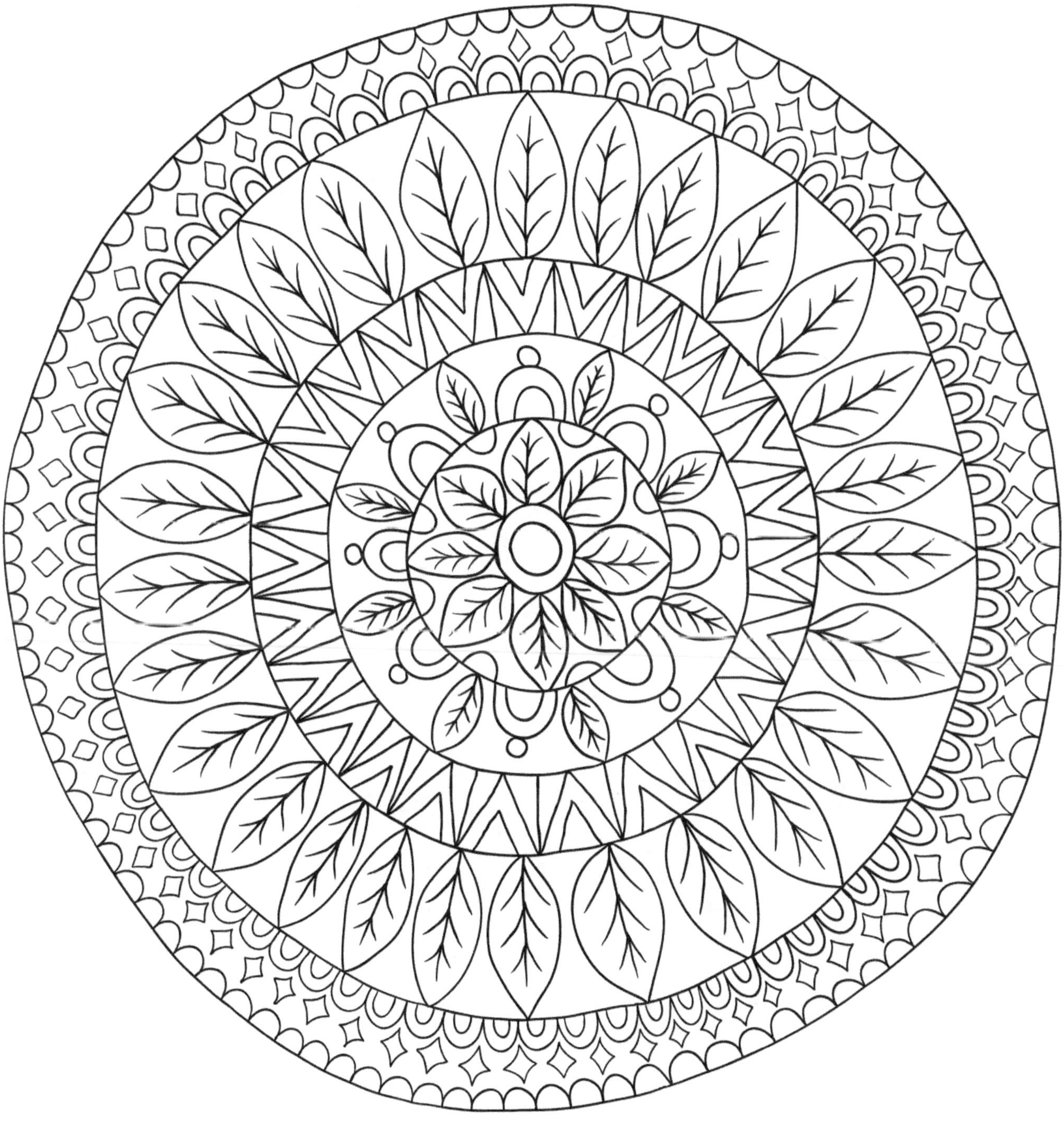

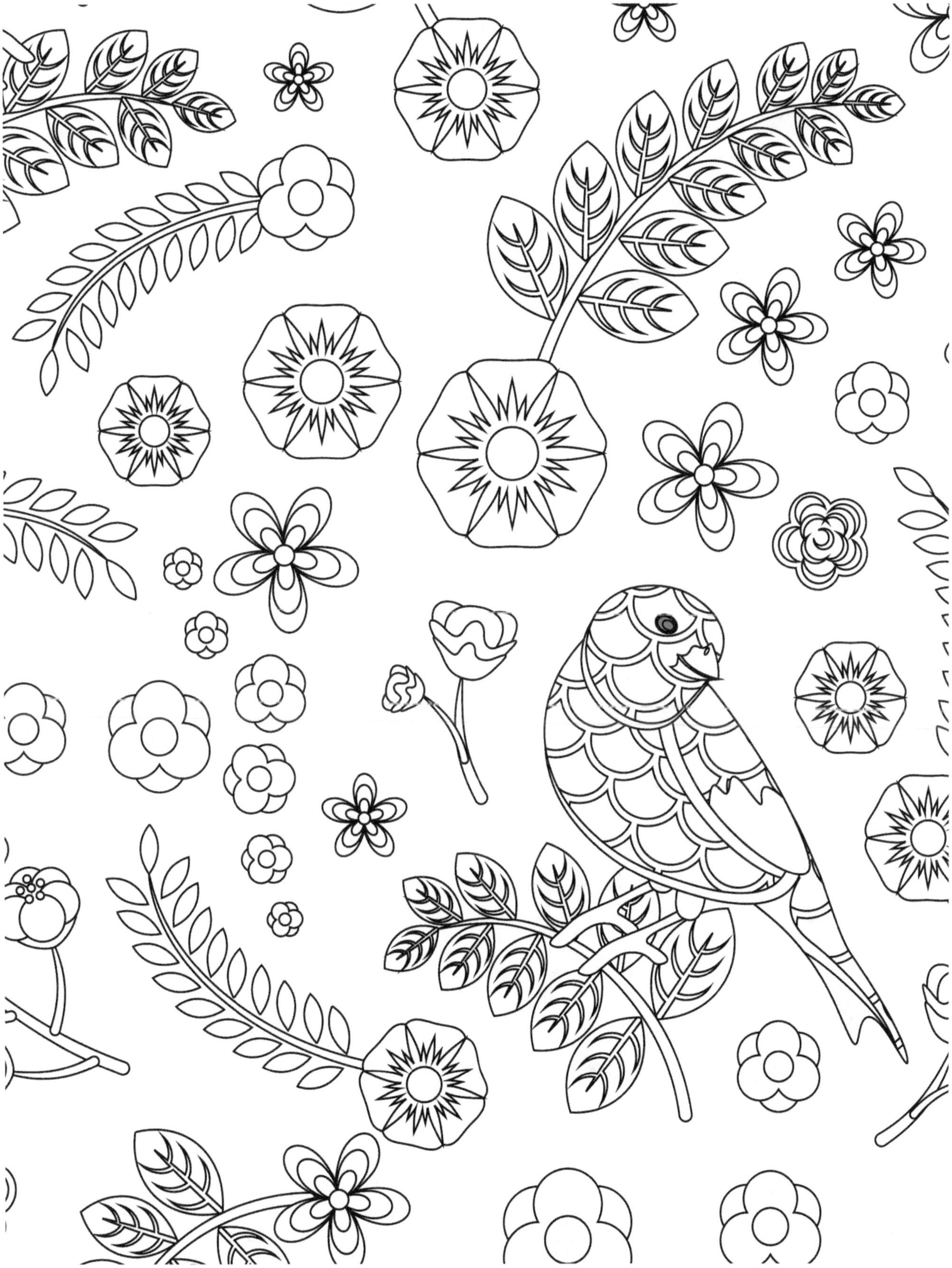

LOVED THIS BOOK?

Share us your colorful artwork!
http://www.KymieEdwins.com

/Kymie-Edwins @KymieEdwins @KymieEdwins

www.ingramcontent.com/pod-product-compliance
Lightning Source LLC
Chambersburg PA
CBHW080642180526
45168CB00008B/3276